# LIVING WITH GRIEF

# Living with Grief

Nicholas Wolterstorff

CASCADE *Books* • Eugene, Oregon

LIVING WITH GRIEF

Cascade Books
An Imprint of Wipf and Stock Publishers
199 W. 8th Ave., Suite 3
Eugene, OR 97401

www.wipfandstock.com

PAPERBACK ISBN: 979-8-3852-0100-6
HARDCOVER ISBN: 979-8-3852-0101-3
EBOOK ISBN: 979-8-3852-0102-0

*Cataloguing-in-Publication data:*

Names: Wolterstorff, Nicholas, author.

Title: Living with grief / Nicholas Wolterstorff.

Description: Eugene, OR : Cascade Books, 2024 | Includes bibliographical references and index.

Identifiers: ISBN 979-8-3852-0100-6 (paperback) | ISBN 979-8-3852-0101-3 (hardcover) | ISBN 979-8-3852-0102-0 (ebook)

Subjects: LCSH: Bereavement—Psychological aspects | Grief—Religious aspects—Christianity.

Classification: BV4905.3 .W65 2024 (paperback) | BV4905.3 .W65 (ebook)

*To the students enrolled in the*
*Calvin Prison Initiative,*
*men behind bars*
*in the Handlon Correctional Facility,*
*by whom I have been*
*moved, instructed, and honored.*

# CONTENTS

# PRELUDE

My little book *Lament for a Son* (1987) was a cry of grief. Not a *discourse about* grief—a cry *of* grief. And not a generic cry of grief. *My* cry of grief over the early death of *my* dear son Eric in a mountain-climbing accident in 1983.

Elizabeth Kübler-Ross is well-known for introducing the idea of stages of grief. She identified five stages that, so she claimed, are typical of persons in grief: denial, anger, bargaining, depression, and acceptance. Some writers have identified a stage before denial, namely shock, and a stage after acceptance, namely processing.

My grieving, like all grieving, changed over time—call those changes "stages" if you wish. But if the stages Kübler-Ross identified are indeed typical, my grieving was not typical. I did not experience denial; I did not experience anger; I did not engage in bargaining; I did not become depressed. Dominant in my grieving, after the initial shock had subsided, was acceptance—pained, tearful, immobilizing acceptance of my loss and of my grief over my loss. At first, the grief was always present, up front, intense. Then, gradually, it receded and became episodic.

When I composed *Lament for a Son*, the words of my cry came to me. I did not search for words. The words came unbidden, mysteriously, and I took them down. They are unlike anything else I have written before or since. Many of them are highly imagistic. "I buried myself that warm June day. It was me over whom we shoveled dirt" (35). "Sorrow is no longer the islands but the sea" (47). "Your tears are salve on [my] wound, your silence is salt" (35). The text consists of fragments. I tried for a time to connect the fragments, but they resisted connection. My life had been fractured; my cry would have to be fractured as well. The ample white space between the fragments represents silence. Faced with death, we should not talk much.

I could not write *Lament* today. I am no longer in grief and no longer cry out in grief. Now I experience grief over Eric's death only on those occasions when, unanticipated, it briefly flares up. Anything in my experience, no matter how innocuous—a chance remark, a piece of clothing, a work of art—bears the potential of triggering a train of associations that culminates in renewed grief. Then it's gone; the flare-up is over. But the memory of being in grief remains, and the loss. The loss does not go away; it will never go away. Eric is forever gone. I have to live with that reality. This present book, written thirty-five years after *Lament*, tells of how I have come to live with the loss that will never go away and with my memory of being in grief over that loss.

The "I" of *Lament*, the self crying out, was the self of a Christian—a Christian with theological convictions, questions, and perplexities, by profession a philosopher. The self of this present book is that same self. It tells of the questions I have asked, the answers I have settled on, the perplexities that remain. What is this excruciatingly painful intrusion into my life, this grief over loss? How do I live around this gap in my life, the gap where Eric once was? And where is God in all this? Who is God? Is God still love? I have not "gone it alone" in asking these questions and searching for answers; I have looked for guidance and wisdom in the long tradition of Christian thought.

Over the years since the publication of *Lament* I have given a few talks on living with grief. The talks have been brief—forty-five minutes or so. In most cases, I played down the theology so as to make what I said accessible to a wider audience. I have given such talks only on request; I have never volunteered them. Rather often, members of the audience would come up to me afterward and suggest that I publish the text of my talk. Each time I stalled. On one occasion, a member of the audience suggested that I take my talk on a speaking tour. I found the prospect repulsive.

The lengthiest talks I have given on the topic, and the most overtly theological, were three lectures I addressed to faculty and students of Fuller Theological Seminary in January 1993, under the sponsorship of the Fuller Symposium on the Integration of Faith and Psychology. Again, members of the audience came up to me afterwards and strongly urged me to publish the text of my talk. Again, I stalled.

Why have I stalled? Listeners told me they found what I had said helpful in their own struggle to live with loss and grief and would like to have my words in hand. Why did I resist their urging? Why not do what they asked?

I have never fully understood my reluctance; but mainly I think it was because I felt that if I elaborated beyond a forty-five minute talk how I have come to live with loss and grief, I would have few readers. As mentioned above, I am a philosopher by profession, with theological questions and convictions. That would show. I feared that most potential readers would find the description of my way of living with loss and grief too theological, too philosophical—too cerebral for their taste, too much head and not enough heart. *Lament for a Son* was a cry of the heart; *Living with Grief* would be descriptive, reflective. *Lament for a Son* is only implicitly theological; *Living with Grief* would be overtly so. The style would be different, less appealing to most readers. *Lament for a Son* is fragmentary, *Living with Grief* would be continuous. *Lament* is highly imagistic; *Living* would be dry, literal, prosaic.

My good friend Dale Cooper regularly teaches a course on pastoring for the men behind bars in the Richard A. Handlon Correctional Facility who are enrolled as students in the Calvin Prison Initiative. The Calvin Prison Initiative is a program offered by Calvin University (Grand Rapids, Michigan) in Handlon Correctional Facility, located in Ionia, about twenty-five miles east of Grand Rapids. Each year Calvin selects around twenty-five men from prisons around the state as first-year enrollees in a five-year program that culminates in a BA degree. For some years, Cooper has been reading and discussing *Lament for a Son* with his students there; I have participated in a few of those sessions.

Recently he remarked to me that he had happened on a copy of the text of my Fuller lectures in his files (I have lost my own copy, and the text is no longer on my computer) and asked whether he had my permission to distribute copies to the men in his class for reading and discussion. He subsequently reported that the students found what I had written very helpful, and commissioned him to tell me that I must publish the lectures. It was learning that the men behind bars in Handlon found my Fuller lectures helpful, and urged me to publish them, that finally overcame my hesitation and prompted me to revise them for publication under the title *Living with Grief*.

No person's grief is quite like another's; grief is particular. Nonetheless, it was my hope, in publishing *Lament for a Son*, that though the book was my own intensely personal and particular cry of grief over my son's early death, there would be aspects of my cry that others could adapt and appropriate for their own cry of grief. That has proved to be the case.

Just as grief is particular, so too is living with grief; each life-with-grief has its own distinct contour, its own inscape. Accordingly, *Living with Grief* is not a general discourse about the psychology of living with grief but—to say it again—my telling of how I have come to live with *my* grief over *my* son's early death. Though it is, in that way, thoroughly particular, the response of the men in Handlon to the text leads me to expect that there will be other readers who likewise find that they can adapt and appropriate, for their own lives, elements of how I have come to live with my grief over my son's early death.

I have dedicated the book to those men in the Handlon Correctional Facility who are enrolled as students in the Calvin Prison Initiative. The four or five occasions when I have been in class with them have been the most moving educational experiences of my entire career. The men are bright, articulate, and industrious. I have had many such students over the course of my career. What sets these students apart, most of them in prison for life, is that they are adults who speak freely of the crimes they have committed, of the ruin they have wreaked on their own lives and the lives of others, and who openly express their grief. It was in listening to them that I came to realize something I should have realized long ago: a prison is a house of grief.[*]

— JANUARY 2023

[*] Correction: I was a participant in the discussion when the revised draft of *Living with Grief* was discussed by Calvin students in the Richard A. Handlon Correctional Facility. In the course of the discussion, one of the men read this last sentence and then said, "Nick, a prison is not a *house* of grief. A prison is a *warehouse* of grief." I choked up. When I had recovered my composure, I thanked him warmly for his correction. A prison is not a *house* of grief. A prison is a *warehouse* of grief.

ONE  *What Is Grief?*

Almost all of us must cope with the presence of grief in our lives. The grief may be mild or intense, over many losses or few; but cope with grief we must. The only exceptions are those who die young or love little. Dying young or loving little—those are the only ways, in our world, of keeping grief at bay. The rest of us have no choice but to incorporate grief into our way of being in the world.

What is grief? When I was in grief and composing *Lament for a Son*, I understood almost nothing of grief. I knew, of course, that I was suffering, and I realized that had I not loved Eric, I would not be in grief. But that is all I understood.

As the grief subsided, I struggled to understand. What is this intrusion into my life, this excruciatingly painful intrusion? Over and over I returned to the question; I could not leave it alone. I was obsessed. Many who have grieved have not had this obsession, probably most have not. I did. It was, no doubt, the philosopher in me.

It was not a definition of "grief" that I was looking for. One can find that in *Webster's Collegiate Dictionary*. It was an understanding of grief that I wanted. Where, on the map of the human self, do we find grief? At the intersection of which operations, which workings? What were the workings of my human self that plunged me into grief when I received the word that Eric had died?

## Two Systems of Suffering

We find grief where there is suffering; that's obvious. To understand the workings of suffering, we must attend to aspects of our humanity whose location in our existence is deep and pervasive.

The opposite of suffering is joy, delight. In us human beings there are two distinct systems, two distinct operations, that produce suffering and delight. One of these is associated with experience, call it the *experiential* system; the other is associated with belief, call it the *doxastic* system (from the Greek term *doxa*, meaning "belief"). Begin with the experiential system.

Pass before your mind's eye examples of human experience in all its rich variety: sensations, moods, perceptions, emotions, desires, pains, hopes, regrets, beliefs—on and on. And then notice the following fundamental fact about our way of having such experiences. Whereas some are such that having them is a matter of indifference to us, there are many we *like* having and many we *dislike* having. Most of us like the taste of chocolate ice cream; I have never yet come across someone who does not dislike the smell of sulfur. In short, many of our experiences are, as it were, charged—some positively, some negatively, while some lack charge. The charges come in varying degrees of intensity, from intensely positive to intensely negative.

Think, now, of one's experiences as located on a continuum of positive and negative charge. As one moves out from the neutral center toward the positive end, one reaches a point where everything beyond is experienced joyfully. As one moves out from the neutral center toward the negative end, one reaches a point where everything beyond is experienced sufferingly.

Physical pain, for example, is experienced by most of us most of the time with a negative charge—though I recall occasions when I had a slightly sore finger and rather enjoyed pressing the sore spot to feel the pain. When the pain is intense, we experience it sufferingly.

We often speak of someone suffering *from* pain, of someone's suffering being *caused by* depression; similarly, we speak of someone getting delight *from* the music. In speaking thus, we use causal and causal-sounding language to describe the relation between, on the one hand, the suffering or joy, and on the other hand, the experience of pain, depression, or listening to music. It would be a mistake, however, to think of the connection between suffering or joy and some experience as the connection of causality. The suffering that we describe as "caused by" pain is not some distinct suffering-sensation caused by the pain-sensation. When it is the experiential system we are dealing with, suffering and joy are, as it were, adverbial modifiers of experience. They are *ways of having* some experience. Physical pain and mental depression are among the experiences that we typically have sufferingly; listening to music and savoring good food are among the experiences that we often have joyfully. Suffering is an existential No-saying to certain experiences; delight, an existential Yes-saying.

Let us move on from these observations about the workings of the experiential system to some observations about the workings of what I call the *doxastic* system. When I learned of the death of my son, I was plunged into suffering. What caused my suffering was not his death; in the interim of a few days between his death and my learning of it, I was not suffering. What caused my suffering was my coming to believe that he was dead. If things had gone in the opposite way, if I had come to believe he was dead when he was not, I would also have been plunged into suffering. Our beliefs have the power of casting us into suffering whether or not they are true.

What I suffered over was not, however, the experiential phenomenon of my believing that my son was dead; it was over my son's death that I suffered. It was the *content* of my belief that I suffered over, *what I believed to be the case*, not my act of believing. I did not suffer from the believing itself. The suffering that occurs when the experiential system is operating is suffering that consists of sufferingly having some experience. The suffering that occurs when the doxastic system is operating is suffering whose object is some dire event that one believes to have occurred, whether or not it did. What strange creatures we are!

There are cases in which a person does sufferingly or joyfully experience believing something. A person wracked by religious doubt who finally comes to believe confidently in her salvation not only rejoices over her salvation but also joyfully experiences her confident believing. My case was not like that. My suffering was not my existential No-saying to my *believing* that my son was dead; it was my existential No-saying to my son's death.

Just as the experiential system produces both joy and suffering, so too the doxastic system. I rejoice upon hearing and believing a report about some accomplishment of one of my children. It's over their accomplishment that I rejoice, not over my act of hearing and believing the report of their accomplishment. And I rejoice whether or not the report is true.

## Grief Is Where Love Is

A person in grief is suffering. After noting that there are two distinct systems in the human self that yield suffering—the experiential system and the doxastic system—we saw that the suffering of a person in grief is a yield of the doxastic system. We are cast into grief by coming to believe that something dire has happened, more precisely, by the content of the belief, not by the act of believing itself—cast into suffering by *what* we believe.

Grief is not the only such suffering, however; intense regret for something one has done is also located there, as is intense disappointment over some failure on one's part. We must continue in our quest for the dynamics of grief.

From the moment I was able to stand back and reflect on my grief, I realized that essential to grief is love. Had I not loved Eric, I would not have been in grief over his death. Grief is the price I paid for my love.

Love comes in different forms. There is the love that consists of seeking to promote or sustain the good of some person or living thing; call it *love as benevolence*. In the Greek original of the New Testament, the term for benevolence is *agape*. When the gospels report Jesus as enjoining us, in the second love command, to love our neighbors as ourselves, the term used is *agape*. There is, secondly, the love that consists of being drawn to someone or something because of their excellence; call it *love as attraction*. It is love as attraction that one expresses when one says, for example, "I love Handel's *Messiah*" or "I loved last night's display of the northern lights." There is, third, the love that consists of finding enjoyment in some activity, for example, loving playing the piano, loving gardening, loving woodworking; call such love *activity love*. And fourth, there is the love that consists of being attached to someone or something: to one's children, one's spouse, one's pet, one's house; call this *love as attachment*. Two or more of these different forms of love are often combined, as in friendship.

Love as attachment is mysterious. I may acknowledge that your cat is finer than ours. No matter. Ours is the one I found huddled on our doorstep one cold winter morning, shivering and meowing piteously. I took it in, warmed it, fed it, cared for it. I became attached—bonded. When we become attached to someone or something we often begin to notice good and excellent features that previously we had overlooked. Attachment opens our eyes and hearts to what is praiseworthy. We find ourselves experiencing love as attraction.

It is love as attachment that makes us vulnerable to grief. When our attempts at benevolence fail for some reason, we typically feel frustration, disappointment, not grief. When the object of our love as attraction changes, so that we are no longer attracted, we typically feel not grief but regret. If I could no longer listen to the *Messiah*, could no longer watch the northern lights, I would feel regret. A person is cast into grief when someone or something to which they are attached is lost to them. In *Lament* I wrote, "Out of myself I traveled on a journey of love and attached this self of mine to Eric, my son. Now he's gone, lost, ripped loose from love; and the ache of loss sinks down, and down, deep down into my soul. How deep do souls go?" (49).

Attachment manifests itself in desires and commitments with respect to the one loved. Some of those are desires for one's own wellbeing; we find delight in the company of the one we love. Reflecting on the grief he felt over the death of his teen-age friend, Augustine wrote that the presence of his friend had been "sweeter to me than all the joys of life as I lived it then" (*Confessions*, IV.4). But many of those desires and commitments are for the well-being of the beloved. We want our *children* to flourish; we don't just prize their contribution to *our* flourishing. We invest ourselves in them, doing what we can to promote their flourishing, rejoicing with them over their achievements and the good things that come their way, sorrowing with them over their failures, their disappointments, their broken bones. We invest ourselves in the flourishing of the beloved for *their* sake, not just for *our* sake. We love them as we love ourselves.

Our desires and commitments change over the years. In *Lament for a Son* I wrote:

A child comes into the world weak and vulnerable. From the first minutes of its life, we protect it. It comes into the world without means of sustenance. Immediately we the parents give it of our own. It begins to display feelings and thoughts of its own. We celebrate those and out of our own way of being in the world try to shape and direct and guide them. We give of ourselves to the formation of this other, from helplessness to independence, trying our best to match our mode of giving to the maturing of the child—our giving maturing with the child's maturing. We take it on ourselves to stay with this helpless infant all the way so that it has a future, a future in which we can delight in its delight and sorrow in its sorrow. Our plans and hopes and fears are plans and hopes and fears for it. Along the way we experience the delights and disappointments of watching that future take shape, from babblings to oratory, from flounderings to climbing, from dependence to equality. (57)

My heart was ripped out of me. My desires with respect to Eric, my commitments, my hopes, my expectations—they were no more. My expectation that he would be home for the summer was no more. My plan to attend his graduation was no more. For a month or so I caught myself still planning to do things with him, still expecting him to call. As I was carrying some boxes of his books into the house I heard him say, "Dad, I'm back!" But he was not back.

Eventually the realization sank in, all the way down, that he was dead. I had to learn to live around the gap and with my grief. Loss and grief were not just new additional components in my life. I had to live a different life, a life for which I had neither preparation nor practice. My investment in the flourishing of my son had been woven into the fabric of my life. Now "senseless" was scrawled across it in big black letters. Grief-infused loss destroys meaning.

Loss from which grief ensues takes many forms. My focus here is on the death of the beloved. But sometimes the one loved does not die but becomes alienated. And sometimes they change in such a way that everything one found lovable in them is gone; the ravages wreaked by Alzheimer's disease is a familiar example. I shall never forget the woman who came up to me after a talk I had given on living with grief and whispered to me that her loss was the shattering of all the hopes and dreams she'd had for her son; she had been forced to acknowledge that they would never be realized. She slipped away without elaborating. And then there is what one might call *anticipatory* grief: grief over the anticipated death of the beloved, of a parent in hospice.

And it's not just over the loss of loved ones that we grieve. We grieve over the destruction of our reputation, over the failure of a business that we founded and worked hard to build up, over being fired by a firm to which we had devoted thirty years of faithful service, over the family home going up in flames. The grief of prisoners is over many losses at once, intensifying the grief.*

## Wanting, Not Wishing

Let me describe an image that came to mind over and over when I was in grief. I take my description from the manuscript

---

* This was called to my attention by one of the men in Handlon Prison who participated in the discussion there of the penultimate draft of *Living with Grief*.

for *Lament for a Son*; it does not appear in the published text because the editor found it obscure and thought it best to delete it. I did not disagree. But my interpretation of the image makes an important point about the nature of grief better than anything in the published text.

> Over and over the horse rears up, fighting wildly, desperately, against the bit in its mouth. Each time the rider pulls back with all his strength on the reins, horse's mouth a blur of foam and blood, rider's face and body tense in sweating horror, until both collapse, exhausted.

I rode ponies when I was a teenager; never did I experience anything like this.

What did it mean? At the time, I had no idea; I think I now know. It's a symbolic representation of a contradiction at the heart of grief.

I remember, as a teenager, wishing to be a major-league baseball pitcher—not just an average pitcher, one of the very best, a twenty-game winner. I fantasized about it. But the fact that my wish was not realized has caused me no disappointment whatsoever. The reason is that it wasn't something I really wanted. I didn't like playing baseball; I had no talent for it. I took no steps whatsoever toward becoming a pitcher. I wished and fantasized, but did not want. Grief ensues from wanting the loved one back, not just wishing. The more intense the wanting, the more intense the grief.

Wanting the loved one back when one knows that is impossible. It has to be knowing or firmly believing that the loss has occurred. Otherwise, what one experiences is not grief but hope—perhaps hope against hope, worried, anxious hope, but nonetheless hope rather than grief. When one knows or firmly believes that the loved one has died, grief ensues from wanting their death to be undone while at the same time knowing that it cannot be undone. Tears and agitation are typical expressions of grief; they are not the thing itself. They're not even necessary. A person can grieve quietly. It's important for family and friends to keep this in mind.

In grief, wanting collides with knowing. I had no doubt that Eric was dead, and I knew there was nothing to be done to restore him to life. But I wanted him to be alive, wanted with every fiber of my being. I did not just wish to talk with him; I wanted to talk with him. I did not just wish to embrace him; I wanted to embrace him. And so forth, on and on. At the heart of grief is the wild frustration of wanting intensely what one knows cannot be—banging one's head against the wall, rearing up and getting pulled back. I was both horse and rider.

It's this collision between wanting and knowing that accounts for the agonized immobility of the person in grief. There is nothing to be done. If you are frightened, you can run away. If you are angry, you can vent your rage. When you are in grief, there is nothing to be done, nothing anyone can do to make happen what you want to happen. You were invested in the one now lost; a whole complex of desires, commitments, hopes, and expectations were centered on them. You cannot turn these off, just like that. Yet there is nothing to be done to achieve your desires, your commitments, your hopes, your expectations. So you don't do anything, except weep and rage, helplessly.

When running away alleviates fear, when lashing out alleviates anger, what happens is that the wanting that is constitutive of the emotion motivates certain actions on one's part, and success in performing those actions alleviates the intensity of the emotion. In the case of grief, there are no actions for the wantings to motivate; there is nothing to be done. The emotion will eventually subside. But for that to happen, there is nothing to be done other than wait. There is nothing to be done to alleviate grief—other than change oneself, if one can, so that one no longer wants one's child to be alive or no longer even thinks about it.

Grief is an irrational emotion. At its heart is wanting what one knows to be impossible, and that's irrational. It makes no sense. It is this irrationality at the heart of grief that leads persons who have not personally experienced grief to say to the person in grief, "Get over it. No use crying over spilled milk. You can't bring him back." And it is the fact that grief is irrational at its core that makes it almost irresistibly tempting, in our society, to regard the person in grief as needing therapy.

We do not regard the fearful person as needing therapy. Of course, some fearful persons are irrationally fearful; but fear is often a healthy and rational response to what one perceives as threatening. If a fearful person comes to one for counsel—counsel as advice rather that counsel as therapy—one first considers whether their view of threat is accurate. Perhaps, when all the facts are laid on the table, it's clear that what they fear is unlikely ever to happen. Or perhaps it's likely to happen if they don't take steps to prevent it; one then explores with them which steps are most likely to be successful. If, on the other hand, it seems that the feared event cannot be prevented, one then explores strategies for minimizing the damages.

Counsel of this sort, call it *advice-counseling*, is an exercise in shared rationality; underlying it is the assumption, usually unspoken, that one should not want things that are impossible. But that assumption is exactly what grief, at its core, violates. And so it is regularly assumed that the grieving person is in need of therapy. The grieving person is to be treated like the irrationally fearful person, like the irrationally jealous person. Grief, so it is assumed, is inherently pathological. One does what one can to return the grieving person to health, to rationality. One tries to get them to stop wanting what cannot be.

Given that there is, at the heart of grief, an irrational collision between what one wants and what one knows, it's easy to understand why this response is so common. But grief as such is no more a disorder to be cured than anger is. Of course, some grief is pathological, just as some anger is pathological. But from the fact that irrationality resides at the heart of grief it does not follow that grief, as such, is pathological. Grief is unlike most emotions in that irrationality is not the proof of pathology. Grief is the normal response, and not only the normal response, but the *appropriate* response, to the irreparable loss of love's object.

Not only is therapy-counseling irrelevant to the grieving person; so too is advice-counseling. One can, as we saw, advise the fearful person by first considering whether their representation of reality is accurate and then, if it is, by reflecting with them on the most sensible strategy to follow for dealing with the threat. But there is nothing for the person grieving over the death of a loved one to do. What they want is that the dead person be alive, and there is nothing anybody can do to bring that about. There is nothing to give advice about.

I realize that some well-meaning religious persons try to alleviate the grief by declaring that the person who has died is not really lost. But this is irrelevant. Believing that one's child or spouse or friend is eternally lost is not typically the cause of grief over their death; if it were, then being convinced that one is mistaken, that one's child or spouse or friend is not eternally lost, would indeed dissipate the grief. What typically causes grief is believing that the person one loves has died, so that all one's desires for their presence in one's life and for their earthly flourishing are now deprived of their object. Being reminded that they remain in the Lord's hand does not bring them back to life.

Normally the grieving person's representation of reality is accurate; the one loved has died, and there is no advice to be given as to how to change that. Advice-counseling is just as irrelevant to the grieving person as therapy-counseling. Rather than counseling her, sit beside her on the mourning bench.

## Why Grief Is Appropriate Even Though Irrational

In discussing the suffering caused by what I called the *experiential system*, I remarked that suffering from physical pain is existential No-saying to the pain, that suffering from mental depression is existential No-saying to the depression, and so forth. Suffering from pain or depression is the crying out by one's existence, "This should not be." It is existential testimony to the evil of severe pain and depression. And severe pain and depression are indeed evils; hence the appropriateness of the suffering.

So, too, for the suffering produced by the doxastic system. Suffering over the death of my son is my No-saying to my son's early death, not just with thought and tongue but with my very existence—with all that is in me. It is my existential crying out, "This should not be." Suffering over the loss of my son is existential testimony to the evil of his death. And his death was indeed an evil. My suffering is the appropriate response to his loss.

To say "no" to my son's death is perforce also to say "yes" to his life, and to my love of his life. My grief is my existential honoring of him; it is my paying existential tribute to his worth and to the worth of my love. My son was, and is, worthy of honor, and my love was, and is, of worth. Let me quote some fine words on the matter from the philosopher Richard Swinburne. "The world is better," he writes,

> if agents pay proper tribute to losses and failures, if they are sad at the failure of their endeavours, mourn for the death of a child, are angry at the seduction of a wife, and so on. Such emotions involve suffering and anguish, but in having such proper feelings a man shows his respect to himself and others. A man who feels no grief at the death of his child or to the seduction of his wife is rightly branded by us as insensitive, for he has failed to pay the proper tribute of feeling to others, to show in his feeling how much he values them, and thereby failed to value them properly—for valuing them properly involves having proper reactions of feeling to their loss.*

These words point to the appropriateness of the *suffering* embedded in grief over the loss of the one loved. A distinct but related question is this: Can we also discern some appropriateness in that irrational phenomenon of *continuing to want* what one knows to be impossible?

The lives of all of us are filled with things around which we orient desires but which are such that, if they are irreparably lost, we would almost immediately give up those desires. We would not bang our head against the wall, wanting them back

---

*Swinburne, *Existence of God*, 192.

while knowing that they cannot be brought back. What kinds of things are these? Things we regard as replaceable. The car I own is the focus of a wide variety of desires on my part; but if it were totaled in a collision, I would be annoyed but not cast into grief. It's insured, so I would not be set back financially. And I can easily get another car that will do what I want even better than my present one does.

My son was not like that; he was not replaceable. All those desires centered on him: I cannot just attach them to someone else. The irrationality that lies at the heart of grief is testimony to the irreplaceability of the one loved.

## Grief Subsides

Grief, I have said, subsides. Though it cannot be relieved or alleviated, it does subside. The way to alleviate grief over the death of a loved one would be to bring the loved one back to life. That's impossible. Sometimes the person in grief learns that she was mistaken in believing that the one she loved was lost. Then the grief vanishes; it does not get alleviated, it disappears. The attention of the griever can be drawn to other things; that too does not alleviate the grief, it distracts the griever.

But grief does subside, slowly, over time. It subsides mostly, I think, because one learns to live around the gap. One has no choice. One lives one's life differently, reorders one's way of investing oneself in the world. For a long time one continues to want to talk with the person one loved, and still loves. But there is nothing one can do to satisfy that desire, no way to embed it within one's ongoing plans. It's irrelevant to one's plans. The result is that slowly the desire becomes less intense, less preoccupying; nothing reinforces it. The same irrationality of grief that at first makes grief so agonizing leads eventually to its subsiding. One notices, after a while, that one is no longer in grief. Though it flares up without notice, one is no longer grieving.

But life is not the same. A person released from prison after torture no longer suffers from the pain of the torture—but they remember. And the world seen through the lens of remembered torture looks different from the world not seen through that lens. The griever's experience is like that, when the grief subsides. The world seen through the lens of remembered grief looks different. In *Lament* I wrote:

The world looks different now. The pinks have become purple, the yellows brown. Mountains now wear crosses on their slopes. Psalms and hymns have reordered themselves so that lines that previously I scarcely noticed now leap out. "The Lord will not suffer thy foot to stumble." Photographs that once evoked the laughter of delighted reminiscence now cause only pain. . . . The pleasure of seeing former students is colored by the realization that they were his friends and that while they thrive he rots. (46)

# INTERLUDE  *What to Say*

Suppose the diagnosis of grief that I have presented is sub-stantially correct. What then should one say—and not say—to a person in grief?

**Say something.** Worst of all is the friend who says nothing; there is nothing so excruciatingly painful as that. I know why some people say nothing. They don't know what to say. They think they should say something wise, something helpful, something that is not a cliché; but they can't think of anything like that, so they say nothing. If you can't think of anything to say, say that you can't think of anything to say, but that you want me to know you are with me in my grief. That's good enough. Or they are afraid that if they say something, they will break down. That's OK; say something and let yourself break down. You don't even have to say it with words. Say it with your body; embrace me. Say something.

**Express your love for the grieving person.** And don't worry whether you are doing so in a wise and eloquent way; express your love. The grieving person will usually know how to penetrate through a haze of clumsy and inept words to the love behind the words.

**Do not downplay the grief.** Do not say that, really, it's not so bad. Unless the grief is misplaced, it is bad. Do not try to console the grieving person. Do not say things like, "You still have four other children, do you not?" You are dealing with a broken human being. A large part of their way of inhabiting the world has been crushed, shattered. That's bad—really bad. Do not say it is not. In my *Lament* I wrote: "If you think your task is to tell me that really, all things considered, it's not so bad, you do not sit with me in my grief but stand off in the distance away from me. Over there, you are of no help. What I need to hear from you is that you recognize how painful it is. I need to hear from you that you are with me in my desperation. To comfort me, you have to come close. Come sit beside me on my mourning bench" (34).

**Do more listening than talking.** Let the grieving person pour out her soul in whatever way she wants. Do not try to stifle her, and do not try to correct her, not at first, anyway. Do not say things like, "You really shouldn't say that" or "You really shouldn't think about it like that." Listen, listen for the suffering, forget about accuracy for the time being. If the grieving person doesn't want to talk, accept that; just be there, for her and with her, like Job's friends.

**You may have to help identify the grief, to help name it.** Sometimes the source of grief is obscure; naming it, identifying it, may prove difficult. I am thinking here of a person who came up to me after a talk I had given on living with grief and said that he had been cast into grief by wrecking his car, and that it took him half a year to figure out what was going on, why he was grieving. It turned out that it was not the car that he was grieving over.

**Offer corrections eventually and gently.** You may conclude that the grief is misplaced, that the thing loved was not worth that much love, or that the loss is not irrevocable. You may even conclude that the grief is pathological. Offer corrections eventually, not immediately, and gently, not in a judgmental tone but in the spirit of a listening love.

**Praise the one loved.** If the love was not misplaced, join in honoring and praising the person or thing. I can testify that such praise is both painful and mysteriously healing. It's painful because it reminds one of all that is lost; it's healing, I think, because if affirms the goodness of one's love.

**Grief isolates.** It's important to realize and keep in mind that grief does not unite, it isolates. The old aphorism has it, "There is company in misery." Not true—not when the misery is grief. Grief makes you turn inward, makes you want to curl up and tune out the world. And if your situation is one of isolation— prison, assisted living for the elderly—the isolation of grief can be almost unbearable.

**Keep in mind that each person's grief has its own pace, and that there is no right or wrong pace.** It is particularly important to remind members of the family of this, since at any given time they will differ in the intensity of their grief. This isolates. "Why is he going briskly about his business when I can barely force myself out of bed?" Occasionally persons have come up to me and asked, "Is it right for me still to be grieving the way I am?" After listening to their description of their griev- ing, I have always replied, "It is right." Their grief has never seemed to me pathological. Grief takes many forms.

**When the occasion seems right, call attention to what remains good in life.** Do not do so by enunciating the ab- straction, "There remain good things in life." Do so by calling attention to good things. "Did you notice the glorious sunset last night?" "Did you hear about Joe's new job?"

**Accept the grieving person's immobility.** This can be diffi- cult, it can wear on one's patience. But do your best to accept it. There is nothing they can do to alleviate the grief.

**Assist them in restructuring their faith.** If the grieving person is a person of faith, they will invariably find that their engagement with Scripture, with hymns, with communal worship has changed. Lines in the psalms to which one had previously paid no attention now leap out: "The Lord will not allow thy foot to stumble" (Psalm 121:3). Verses in hymns that one sang joyfully now sound glib, and the singing, too boisterous. Do what you can to help the grieving person cope with these changes.

**Do not say that you know what it's like, because you don't.** I'm not sure why I found it painful when people said this to me, but I did. If it was someone who had also lost a child, I could accept it. But coming from others, no. I had the sense that my grief was being diminished, perhaps because their comment generalized my grief. Grief is particular, more particular than anything else in our existence. Grief resists generalization. Each of us has, at best, a glimpse of what the other person's grief is like.

# TWO   *Owning and Disowning Loss and Grief*

How do we deal with loss that casts us into grief, and with our grief over that loss? That is a question we all face, all who do not die young or love little. It was the question I faced when I began to recover from the immobility that assaulted me upon learning of Eric's death.

In the course of my struggle to answer the question I took note of how others around me were dealing with their loss and grief, and I read how some, in the past, had dealt with theirs. What I saw, many times over, was the attempt to *disown* loss and grief.

I could not go down that road. I felt intuitively that to disown my loss and grief would be a profound dishonoring both of my son and of my love of him. I would struggle to *own* my loss and my grief. The best way to explain what I mean by *owning* is to describe some common ways of *disowning*, and then take note of how owning differs from those. Let me identify three ways in which people try to disown their loss and grief, and why they do so.

## The Narratival Disowning of Loss and Grief

When I listened, I heard people speak of "getting over" grief, of "putting one's grief behind" one, of "getting on with life." "No use crying over spilled milk," they said. This is the language of disowning. More specifically, it is the language of what I call the *narratival* disowning of loss and grief.

When I was a professor, and a new student came to my office with some questions they wanted to ask, I would usually say, "Before we get to your questions, tell me who you are." Open-ended though my request was, and strange as it may have sounded to some, the answer they gave was always of the same sort; they narrated that part of their lives which they thought would be helpful for me to know about.

Each of us is constantly engaged in constructing a more or less coherent narrative of our lives. We assign great significance to some events, to others minor significance, and we allow yet others to be forgotten. These narratives are constantly being revised. We incorporate the new things we do and the new things that happen to us, recall things we had forgotten, allow others to recede from memory, come to see earlier episodes in a new light.

That last point is important. Our life-narratives change not only because there is constantly more to tell but also because later episodes lead us to see earlier episodes differently. Some of these are changes in the eyes of the beholder. We have all said to ourselves something like, "Only recently did I realize that what I had been doing all along was trying to live up to my father's expectations." But some are changes in the things themselves; later episodes alter the significance of earlier episodes. "What happened a year after I applied for the position made the rejection of my application insignificant."

A reasonably accurate and coherent life-narrative is one of the most valuable things a person can have. They guide us in our decisions, shape our relationships, give birth to our hopes and fears. They give meaning to our lives; life is not just one thing after another.

The narratival disowning of loss and grief consists of the role one gives to loss and grief in the composition of one's life-narrative. The aim is to reach the point where one no longer regards them as significant—to reach the point where one seldom recalls one's loss and grief, or, if one does, they no longer carry any emotional resonance. When one tells someone the story of one's life, one doesn't bother to mention them.

"But didn't you have a wife who died of cancer when she was still in her thirties?"

"Yes, you're right, I did; but it didn't occur to me to mention it; I hardly ever think about it any more. But now that you remind me, yes."

It's not only loss and grief that we try to disown narratively. Each of us experiences a good many painful or unpleasant things in the course of our lives that we disown in this way—incidents of being bullied when we were in grade school, for example. At the time, we were deeply angry and upset; now, we have either forgotten the episodes or, if we happen to recall them, we do so without emotion.

It's not hard to see why one would be content to let episodes of being bullied in grade school fade from memory. But why the death of someone one loved, and one's grief over their death? Why would anyone disown those? I suggest that the narratival disowning of loss and grief is intertwined, as both cause and consequence, with the remarkable technological advances of modern society.

We in the modern world are habituated to respond to the occurrence in experience or environment of something we dislike by altering the experience or changing the environment so that the object of our dislike is removed. We are habituated to being in control. Human beings have, of course, always done some of this. What plants the habit so deeply in us, and disposes us to employ it so pervasively, is the remarkable successes we have had. Headaches are annoying or painful, so we take aspirin. High heat and humidity are uncomfortable, so we turn on the air conditioning. Our friends are too far away to be able to talk face-to-face, so we pick up the phone. The death of children from childhood diseases was a common source of grief in earlier days, so we vaccinate. A business that de-

pends on the happenstance preferences of potential custom-
ers is precarious, so it buys advertising designed to manipulate
preferences. Though wool is warm, it's also rather heavy, so we
develop those warm but lightweight materials now made into
jackets and sold by L. L. Bean and Patagonia. The list goes on
and on. I agree with those critics of modernity who argue that
this whole pattern of action produces its own budget of sorrows
and sufferings. But the project as a whole has been stunningly
successful; no one wishes it all to be undone. All that any of
us wish for is the ability to pick and choose—to get rid of the
advertising, say, but keep the vaccines.

Though our degree of success is stunning, we are nowhere
near wholly successful, nor will we ever be. We are not, and never
will be, fully in control. Suffering can be diminished; it cannot
be eliminated. Indeed, technology offers not only new ways of
alleviating suffering but also new ways of causing suffering; those
with an impulse toward cruelty find new means at their disposal.
We in the modern world are remarkably successful in holding
loss at bay; but loss does come, and grief along with it. There will
always be the death of loved ones and the grief that ensues.

The death of a person one loves is an unmistakable example of not being in control. So, too, the frustration of wanting
the impossible, which lies at the heart of grief. Rather than being in control, the person in grief has been assaulted. I suggest
that it is in good measure the relentless desire to be in control,
and to see oneself as being in control, that drives our attempts
to disown loss and grief narratively. One can regard oneself as

being in control, or one can openly acknowledge one's loss and grief: one cannot do both.

Perhaps there is another dynamic as well that drives our attempt to disown loss and grief narratively, different but related. Over the ages, human beings have developed habits and rituals for coping with suffering, passing these on from generation to generation. Those habits and rituals have broken down among us, in part, at least, because of our success in alleviating suffering in our part of the world. So when loss and grief do pierce our armor and assault us, we try for amnesia, not knowing what else to do, having lost the cultural memory of ways of coping.

༄

I could not engage in the narratival disowning of my loss and grief. I could not aim to reach the point where, when telling the story of my life to myself and others, I did not think it worth mentioning my love of Eric, and his death, and my subsequent grief. It would be dishonest. A big piece of my heart had been ripped out of me. It would be a lie to consign that to insignificance, and a profound dishonoring, both of my son and of my love of him. If he was worth loving when alive, how could he not be worth grieving over when dead? He was a great good in my life, as was my love of him; his death was a great evil. In the story of my life that I compose I shall honor him and my love of him by telling of my loss and of my grief. I shall refuse to make my life-narrative a story of being in control. I was not in control. I was assaulted.

## The Ethical Disowning of Grief

Within the tradition of the Christian church, reaching back into antiquity, there is another way of dealing with grief than the way that is common in contemporary Western society. It, too, is a disowning, but of a very different sort. Call it the *ethical* disowning of grief. With respect to this form of disowning, no need for us to do the work of analysis; it's been done for us, long ago, by Augustine (born 354, died 430).

Augustine's dearest boyhood friend died when Augustine was eighteen. In his *Confessions*, written when he was in his early forties (397–98), Augustine recalls his response. Let me quote him at some length:

> My heart grew somber with grief, and wherever I looked, I saw only death. My own country became a torment and my home a grotesque abode of misery. All that we had done together was now a grim ordeal without him. My eyes searched everywhere for him, but he was not there to be seen. I hated all the places we had known together, because he was not in them and they could no longer whisper to me, "Here he comes!" as they would have done had he been alive but absent for a while. (IV.4)
>
> I lived in a fever, convulsed with tears and sighs that allowed me neither rest nor peace of mind. My soul was a burden, bruised and bleeding. It was tired of the man who carried it, but I found no place to set it down to rest. Neither

the charm of the countryside nor the sweet scents of a garden could soothe it. It found no peace in song or laughter, none in the company of friends at table or in the pleasures of love, none even in books or poetry. Everything that was not what my friend had been was dull and distasteful. I had heart only for sighs and tears. For in them alone I found some shred of consolation. . . . Where could my heart find refuge from itself? Where could I go, yet leave myself behind? (IV.7)

Powerful, astonishing words: My soul "was tired of the man who carried it, but I found no place to set it down to rest."

We, in our day, find Augustine at his most appealing in passages such as these; the intense passion of this extraordinary man from late antiquity, and the gripping eloquence of his rhetoric, draw us irresistibly. And to those of us who have experienced grief similar to that of Augustine, the passage has the mysterious balming effect of expressing with precision our own emotions. All the places that once whispered, "Here he comes," have lost their voice and fallen achingly silent.

We experience a rough jolt, then, when we read further and discover that those very episodes that are, for us, Augustine at his most appealing, were for him, from the time of his conversion onward, the most disgusting. Around a decade before he wrote the passage quoted, thus a good many years after his friend's death, Augustine became a Christian (386). He tells his readers that his reason for recalling his adolescent grief was to confess to God the sin of having loved his friend in such a way that he was cast into grief by his friend's death. "Why do I talk of these things?" he asks. He answers: "It is time to confess, not to question" (IV.6).

Augustine's mother, a devout Christian all her life, died a few years after his conversion. His conversion made his response to his mother's death profoundly different from his response to his friend's death. The passion is still there; but the attitude is different. "I closed her eyes," he writes,

> and a great wave of sorrow surged into my heart.... It would have overflowed in tears if I had not made a strong effort of will and stemmed the flow, so that the tears dried in my eyes.... What a terrible struggle it was to hold them back! As she breathed her last, the boy Adeodatus [Augustine's son] began to wail aloud and only ceased his cries when we all checked him.... I, too, felt that I wanted to cry like a child, but a more mature voice within me, the voice of my heart, made me keep my sobs in check, and I remained silent. (IX.12)

On that earlier occasion, "tears alone were sweet to [him], for in [his] heart's desire they had taken the place of [his] friend" (IV.4). He asked why that was so, "why tears are sweet to the sorrowful." How "can it be that there is sweetness in the fruit we pluck from the bitter crop of life, in the mourning and the tears, the wailing and the sighs?" (IV.5). Now, on the occasion of his mother's death, he "fought against the wave of sorrow" (IX.12).

He did not succeed. After the funeral, as he lay in bed remembering the mother he loved dearly, "the tears which I had been holding back streamed down, and I let them flow as freely as they would, making of them a pillow for my heart. On them it rested . . . (IX.12). "I thought of her devoted love for you [God], and the tenderness and patience she had showed to me, like the holy woman that she was. Of all this, I found myself suddenly deprived. And it was a comfort to me to weep for her and for myself, and to offer my tears to you [God] for her sake and for mine." So now, he continues, "I make you [God] my confession. . . . Let any man read it who will. . . . And if he finds that I sinned by weeping for my mother, even if only for a fraction of an hour, let him not mock at me . . . but weep himself, if his charity is great. Let him weep for my sins to you" (IX.12).

The sin for which Augustine invites the person of charity to weep was not so much the sin of weeping over the death of his mother as the sin of which that weeping was the symptom. I was, he says, "guilty of too much worldly affection" (IX.12).*

This is extraordinary: guilty of too much worldly affection

---

* "You knew, O Lord, how I suffered, but my friends did not, and as they listened intently to my words, they thought that I had no sense of grief. But in your ears, where none of them could hear, I blamed myself for my tender feelings. I fought against the wave of sorrow and for a while it receded, but then it swept upon me again with full force. It did not bring me to tears and no sign of it showed in my face, but I knew well enough what I was stifling in my heart. It was misery to feel myself so weak a victim of these human emotions, although we cannot escape them, since they are the natural lot of mankind, and so I had the added sorrow of being grieved by my own feelings, so that I was tormented by a twofold agony" (Augustine, *Confessions* IX.12).

in his love for his mother, the symptom of his guilt being the grief he felt upon her death! Augustine is embarrassed by his sin. He manages to conceal the symptoms in public. But back in his room he is overwhelmed and breaks down in sobs, finding his tears a pillow for his heart. Now, as he discloses this sin, along with a number of others, to his readers, he pleads with them to regard him with charity rather than condescending judgmentalism.

Clearly a disowning of grief is going on here. But it is not the narratival mode of disowning, in which one tries to reach the point where one's loss and grief no longer have a significant place in one's life-narrative. Augustine most emphatically did incorporate his losses and his grievings into his life-narrative. The Augustinian mode of disowning is what I call the *ethical* mode. Augustine assigns his grief to the old sinful self that he is trying to reform and asks for God's forgiveness and the empathy of his fellows. In the life-narrative that he composes, Augustine tells of the grief he has experienced under the category: *symptom of sinful love.*

The Augustinian attitude became deeply embedded in the Christian tradition. Many are the Christians, down through the ages, who have felt guilty for grieving and who, like Augustine, have done their best to stifle and conceal their grief. Too much worldly affection. Weak faith. If I were detached from that which has only temporal significance, and attached to that which has eternal significance, I would not grieve. Listen again to Augustine:

We did not think it right to mark my mother's death with weeping and moaning, because such lamentations are the usual accompaniment of death when it is thought of as a state of misery or as total extinction. But she had not died in misery nor had she wholly died. Of this we were certain, both because we knew what a holy life she had led and also because our faith was real and we had sure reasons not to doubt it. (IX.12)

What was it in Augustine's line of thought that led him to this way of incorporating grief into his life-narrative—this ethical disowning way? Part of the answer is that Augustine shared with the Platonists of antiquity the conviction that it is our nature to love. We can choose what to love; we cannot choose whether to love.

When Augustine spoke of love, what did he have in mind? I know of no passage in which he explains. But it's clear, just from the passages quoted, that part of what he had in mind is what I called, in chapter 1, *love as attraction*: being in the grip of something, drawn to it, attracted to it, on account of some excellence that it possesses. What is likewise clear from the passages quoted is that he also had in mind what I called *love as attachment*; he was attached to his boyhood friend and to his mother—intensely attached. Augustinian love is a blend of love as attraction and love as attachment.

Another part of the answer to our question, what it was in Augustine's line of thought that led to his ethical disowning of grief, is that Augustine shared with most writers of antiquity the assumption that all human beings are in search of what was called, in Greek, *eudaimonia*, commonly translated into English as "happiness."* There were, as one would expect, disagreements as to what exactly constitutes happiness and how it is to be attained. The view of the Stoics, which Augustine shared, was that a condition of happiness is tranquility, freedom from negative emotions. He writes: our goal is to "attain the things that make us happy and rest in them" (*On Christian Doctrine* I.3.3). Happiness goes beyond tranquility to include delight and joy, but the ground floor of happiness is tranquility.

And how, in Augustine's view, do we attain tranquility? By how we direct our love. By loving that which cannot fail us. And that is God, and God alone; God alone cannot change on us, cannot die. The famous opening sentence of the *Confessions* reads: "Our souls are restless, Lord, until they rest in thee." To love anything other than God is to court disturbance. Many are the passages in which Augustine makes the point. He writes: the soul that "clings to [mutable] things of beauty . . . only clings to sorrow." God alone "is the place of peace that cannot be disturbed. . . . [So] stand with him and you shall not fall, rest in him and peace shall be yours" (IV.11–12). Addressing his own soul, Augustine writes, "[In God] is the place of peace that

* Perhaps better translations into present-day English are "well-being" and "flourishing." But I will follow customary practice and translate it as "happiness."

cannot be disturbed. . . . Make your dwelling in him, my soul. Entrust to him whatever you have" (IV.11).

We have identified the line of thought that led Augustine to advocate the ethical disowning of grief over the death of friends, parents, children, etc. But we would do an injustice to Augustine if we did not take note of another dimension of his thought about the place of grief in our lives, a dimension that complicates things.

Over and over Augustine affirms that love of God, and only love of God, is grief-proof. He does not say, however, that only God is to be loved. That is what one would expect him to say, given his conviction that happiness is what all human beings desire, given his conviction that tranquility is a condition of happiness, and given his conviction that only love of God is impervious to disappointment.

Recall some sentences quoted earlier: if any man "finds that I sinned by weeping for my mother, even if only for a fraction of a second or an hour, let him not mock at me . . . but weep himself, if his charity is great. Let him weep for my sins to you" (IX.12). He says, in another place, "though everyone wants to be happy," nonetheless "we must not arm ourselves against compassion. There are times when we must welcome sorrow on behalf of others" (III.2). And in another place, "[M]y true brothers are those who rejoice for me in their hearts when they find good in me and grieve for me when they find sin. They are my true brothers because whether they see good in me or evil, they love me still" (IX.4).

What was it that led Augustine to this view, extraordinary for a person of late antiquity? What led him, in spite of the influence of the eudaemonist tradition on his thought, to break with that tradition at this point? It was the influence of the New Testament. Probably he was influenced by some passages in St. Paul; for example, "Rejoice with those who rejoice, and weep with those who weep" (Romans 12:15), and "If one member [of the church] suffers, all suffer together with it; if one member is honored, all rejoice together with it" (1 Corinthians 12:26). But in Book One of *On Christian Doctrine* (I.26.27), written around the same time as the *Confessions*, it becomes clear that something deeper is going on than the influence of scattered biblical passages. Augustine found himself confronted with Christ's injunction to "love the Lord your God with all your heart and soul and mind and to love your neighbor as yourself." It was Christ's injunction to love not only God but one's neighbor as oneself that roiled the waters of Augustine's eudaimonism.

How did Augustine fit it all together—the conviction that we all desire tranquility and that it is only in our love of God that we can be assured of tranquility, with the conviction that, out of love for neighbor and self, we are to grieve over our own sin and that of our neighbors? He fitted it together by contrasting this present life with the life to come. In the life to come, there will be no sin over which to grieve; the tranquility for which we long will be enjoyed in full. In this present life, we strive for the tranquility that ensues from loving God and the tranquility that ensues from no longer loving friends and relatives in such a way as to be cast into grief over their deaths.* But we do not strive for the tranquility of being indifferent to sin, our own and others. Quite the opposite; in this present life, we are to be united in a solidarity of grief over sin.

⤺

I could not engage in the ethical disowning of my grief. Augustine spoke with deep affection of "the beloved service" his mother had given him and of "the tenderness and patience she had shown him"; she had been "so precious and so dear to" him that "her life and [his] had been as one" (*Confessions* IV.12). That was Augustine's heart speaking. His head told him that in his attachment to his mother he had been guilty of "too much worldly affection." His mother was not worth such love.

What we find in Augustine, and in the long tradition of Christian piety that he helped to form, is a comprehensive demoting of the worth of flesh-and-blood human beings. On all the grief that ensues from the death of those we love, Augustine pronounces a "no" to the love rather than a "no" to their death. Thereby he also pronounces a "not much" concerning the worth of the one loved. Flesh-and-blood human beings are not worth a love that bears the potential of grief—only the religious and moral condition of their souls is worth such love.

---

* Late in his life, Augustine came to the view that grieving over the death of friends and relatives is not sinful but an expression of our God-given nature. I discuss in considerable detail both Augustine's early view concerning loss and grief and his later view in chapter 8, "Augustine's Break with Eudaimonism," in my *Justice: Rights and Wrongs*.

The religious and moral condition of my son's soul would have been worth grieving over; his death was not.

I could not declare that my son was not worth loving in such a way that his death cast me into grief. God created human beings as creatures who are both animals and persons, personic animals, bearing the image of their creator. Contemplating these extraordinary creatures, God pronounced them "very good." Eric was "very good." He was worth my love. And my grief.

## The Celebration-of-Life Disowning of Loss and Grief

Let me describe a third form of disowning of loss and grief, a form that I find common among present-day Christians. I call it, rather clumsily, the *celebration-of-life disowning*. My description, in this case, can be brief.

The celebration-of-life disowning takes the form of struggling to shape one's emotional life in such a way that one's feelings of grief are suppressed, replaced by feelings of gratitude for what was good in the life of the one loved and by hope for their participation in the life everlasting. Christian funerals are nowadays commonly called "A Celebration of Life." Often no note of grief intrudes into the celebration.

This is not narratival disowning—deleting one's loss and grief from one's life-narrative. Neither is it ethical disowning—confessing to God the sin of too much worldly affection and asking for forgiveness. It is a third, distinct, form of disowning: struggling to shape one's emotional life so that grief is replaced by gratitude and hope.

What is it that motivates this form of disowning? I don't know. The unspoken assumption appears to be that it is somehow religiously wrong, or deficient, to attend to the loss of the one loved and to one's grief over that loss; one should attend instead to what was good in their life, giving thanks to God, and to the hope for life everlasting. But those who engage in this form of disowning do not declare, with Augustine, that they have been guilty of too much worldly affection. In the course of their celebration they openly express their love. So how can it be right to celebrate what was good in a person's life and right to openly express one's love for them, and yet somehow religiously wrong or deficient to grieve over the loss of that good and over the shattering of that love? If my son was worth loving when alive—as he was—then why should I divert attention from my grief when he is dead?

~

I cannot engage in the celebration-of-life disowning of loss and grief. I hear in it a triumphalism that I cannot share: celebrating the *already* and the *to-be* of God's kingdom while ignoring the *not-yet*. I shall indeed celebrate what was good in my son's life; but I shall also grieve over the loss of the good that I celebrate. Celebration intertwined with grief; grief intertwined with celebration.

## Owning Loss and Grief

Augustine stifling his sobs, dissembling to his friends, chastising himself, losing control, confessing to God his sin of too much worldly affection: that is one picture of grief that comes to us from Christian antiquity. Another is this:

> A voice was heard in Ramah,
> > wailing and loud lamentation,
> Rachel weeping for her children;
> > she refused to be consoled,
> because they are no more. (Matthew 2:18)

My model is Rachel, not Augustine.

My grief, given Eric's death, was a good thing, not a sin—existential testimony to the worth of the one I loved and to the worth of my love. Failure to grieve would have been an existential dishonoring of him and of my love. Paradoxical: that this painful intrusion into my life, grief over Eric's death, would be a good thing in my life, given his death.

I will incorporate my loss, and my grief over my loss, into my life-narrative. When someone asks me who I am, I will tell them, perhaps not immediately, but shortly, that I am one who suffered the loss of a dearly loved son at the early age of twenty-five. I will incorporate my grief into my life-narrative as something good and right, not, in the Augustinian way, as something sinful. I will *own* my grief, not disown it—not in the narratival mode, not in the ethical mode, not in the celebration-of-life mode.

Let me quote a passage from Calvin in which he sharply rejects the disowning of grief, and then powerfully affirms owning one's grief. He writes, "Among the Christians there are also new Stoics, who count it depraved not only to groan and weep but also to be sad and care ridden" (*Institutes* III.viii.9). In this, they are seriously mistaken.

> [We are] not to be utterly stupefied and to be deprived of all feeling of pain. Our ideal is not that of what the Stoics of old foolishly described [as] "the great-souled man"; one who, having cast off all human qualities, was affected equally by adversity and prosperity, by sad times and happy ones—nay, who like a stone was not affected at all. (III.viii.9)

The Stoic ideal paints "a likeness of forbearance that has never been found among men, and can never be realized" (III.viii.9). For it is contrary to our created nature.

> Thus afflicted by disease, we shall both groan and be uneasy and pant after health; thus pressed by poverty we shall be pricked by the arrows of care and sorrow; thus we shall be smitten by the pain of disgrace, contempt, injustice; thus at the funerals of our dear ones we shall weep the tears that are owed to our nature. (III.viii.10)

And if there be any doubt that it is indeed our created nature that comes to expression in our grief, not our fallen sinful nature, then the example of Jesus grieving is confirmation. Again I quote Calvin:

> Our Lord and Master has condemned [this iron philosophy] not only by his word, but also by his example. For he groaned and wept both over his own and others' misfortunes. And he taught his disciples in the same way: "The world," he says, "will rejoice but you will be sorrowful and will weep" [John 16:20]. And that no one might turn it into a vice, he openly proclaimed, "Blessed are those who mourn" [Matthew 5:7]. No wonder! For if all weeping is condemned, what shall we judge concerning the Lord himself, from whose body tears of blood trickled down [Luke 22:44]. If all fear is branded as unbelief, how shall we account for that dread with which, we read, he was heavily stricken [Matthew 26:37; Mark 14:33]. If all sadness displeases us, how will it please us that he confesses his soul "sorrowful even to death" [Matthew 26:38]. (III.viii.8)

There are, of course, different ways of owning loss and grief. I have worked to own my loss and grief in a way that I call *redemptive*—to own them in such a way that from this life-fracturing loss, and from my grief over that loss, something good will come. Let me offer, in the Interlude that follows, examples of some of the ways in which loss and grief can be owned redemptively.

INTERLUDE  *Owning Loss and Grief Redemptively*

**We can own our loss and grief redemptively** by reordering our loves and commitments so that they more nearly reflect the true worth of things. Many are the grieving persons who have testified that the loss of someone or something they loved had the effect of making the values by which they had been living look askew. What seemed important now looked trivial, what had been passed by without notice now seemed incredibly dear.

**We can own our loss and grief redemptively** by savoring with renewed intensity and gratitude the good things that come our way, including the small familiar things: a child's laughter, the blue sky, a word of thanks, a pair of ducks. After the assault of loss, the good and beautiful things we had taken for granted look fragile, precarious, in danger of slipping away. We now savor them.

**We can own our loss and grief redemptively** by deepening and expanding our understanding and empathy. At first, grief isolates. But there comes a day when we understand and empathize with others in a way we did not before, especially with those who are also in grief. Never entirely; each person's grief is unique, particular. But solidarity with others blossoms.

**We can own our loss and grief redemptively** by shouting out more loudly than before, "this should not be," at cruelty and injustice, indifference and racism, thereby strengthening in us longing for God's new day. "Blessed are the mourners," said Jesus. What might he have meant? Let me quote from my *Lament*:

> Who . . . are the mourners? The mourners are those who have caught a glimpse of God's new day, who ache with all their being for that day's coming, and who break out into tears when confronted with its absence. They are the ones who realize that in God's realm of [shalom] there is no one blind and who ache whenever they see someone unseeing. They are the ones who realize that in God's realm there is no one hungry and who ache whenever they see someone starving. They are the ones who realize that in God's realm there is no one falsely accused and who ache whenever they see someone imprisoned unjustly. They are the ones who realize that in God's realm there is no one who fails to see God and who ache whenever they see someone unbelieving. They are the ones who realize

that in God's realm there is no one who suffers oppression and who ache whenever they see someone beat down. They are the ones who realize that in God's realm there is no one without dignity and who ache whenever they see someone treated with indignity. They are the ones who realize that in God's realm of [shalom] there is neither death nor tears and who ache whenever they see someone crying tears over death. The mourners are aching visionaries. (85–86)

**We can own our loss and grief redemptively** by expending new energy in working to alleviate the causes of grief and suffering in our world. If we reject the Augustinian attitude, and pay to family and friends the tribute of a love that may suffer, then we will struggle to prolong their lives rather than struggling to reorient our loves so that we are no longer cast into grief by the snuffing out of their lives. If we pay to justice the tribute of a love that may suffer, then we will struggle to reform the systems that oppress and humiliate rather than struggling to reorient our love so that we are indifferent.

**We can own our loss and grief redemptively** by thinking anew about the significance of loss and grief in this world of ours—thinking anew about our customary ways of understanding and coping with loss and grief. If your grief over the death of your child leads you to reject the narratival disowning of loss and grief as an obscene dishonoring of your child and of your love, then you have owned your grief redemptively. If your grief over the death of your mother leads you to reject the Augustinian way of coping with grief as implying a radical dishonoring of the worth of your mother's life and of your devotion to her, then you have owned your grief redemptively.

**Last, we can own our loss and grief redemptively** by entering more deeply into the heart of God. I will develop this thought in the next chapter.[*]

～

"Put your hand into my wounds," said the risen Jesus to Thomas, "and you will know who I am. The wounds of Christ are his identity. They tell us who he is. He did not lose them. They went down into the grave with him and they came up with him—visible, tangible, palpable. Rising did not remove them. He who broke the bonds of death kept his wounds.

To believe in Christ's rising from the grave is to accept it as a sign of our rising from our graves. If for each of us it was our destiny to be obliterated, and for all of us together it was our destiny to fade away without a trace, then not Christ's rising but my dear son's early dying would be the logo of our fate.

---

[*] In the discussion of the penultimate draft of *Living with Grief* by students in the Calvin Prison Initiative in Handlon Correctional Facility, there was an extended discussion of how to live grief redemptively when in prison. I found three comments especially striking: "I can live grief redemptively by doing what I can to help others not do what I did." "I can live grief redemptively by doing what I can to 'fill the holes' in the lives of my fellow prisoners." "I can live grief redemptively by persistent defiance of the system of incarceration."

Slowly I begin to see that there is something more as well. To believe in Christ's rising and death's dying is also to live with the power and the challenge to rise up now from all our dark graves of suffering love. If sympathy for the world's wounds is not enlarged by our anguish, if love for those around us is not expanded, if gratitude for what is good does not flame up, if insight is not deepened, if commitment to what is important is not strengthened, if aching for a new day is not intensified, if hope is weakened and faith diminished, if from the experience of death comes nothing good, then death has won. Then death, be proud.

So I shall struggle to live the reality of Christ's rising and death's dying. In my living, my son's dying will not be the last word. But as I rise up, I bear the wounds of his death. My rising does not remove them. They mark me. If you want to know who I am, put your hand in. (*Lament for a Son*, 92–93)

THREE    *Where Is God in Loss and Grief?*

Our existence is shot through with ambiguity. Is political power good or bad? It all depends on how it is exercised. Often it's exercised abusively, but not always. Is patriotism good or bad? It all depends on what it leads members of the nation to do. Often it proves destructive, but not always. Is religion good or bad? It all depends.

Is suffering like that? Is suffering ambiguous in this same sort of way? Does suffering sometimes aid and sometimes inhibit human flourishing?

## The Ambiguity of Suffering

We have to remember the sort of creatures we are, and the nature of our habitation. Strange boundary-crossing creatures: personic animals endowed with freedom and meant for fellowship with members of our species and with God, placed in a physical world with other animals and forms of life. Daring experiment!

In the first chapter I suggested that there are, in us, two "systems," as I called them, of suffering and joy. One system—I called it the *experiential system*—pertains to the "how" of our having experiences: some experiences we like having, all the way to having them joyfully; some we dislike having, all the way to having them sufferingly; and some we have neutrally. The other system—the *doxastic system*—pertains to belief and conviction. Sometimes our coming to believe that something has happened causes us to delight over that, sometimes it causes us to suffer, and sometimes it leaves us feeling indifferent. We are all created with these two systems.

They are components of the design plan of our constitution *for our life in this physical world*. I feel thirsty; so I drink. I feel hungry; so I eat. I feel a burning sensation in my finger; so I draw back from the hot burner. I feel deeply disappointed over my failure; so I prepare better next time and work harder. If the thirst is severe, the hunger extreme, the pain intense, the disappointment deep, I suffer. The two systems, both when giving us joy and when causing us to suffer, are conducive to our flourishing. Feelings of thirst, hunger, and pain are conducive to our flourishing as animals; feelings of disappointment over failure are conducive to our flourishing as persons.

In light of these considerations, it's obvious that negatively charged experiences in general, and suffering in particular, are not *per se* bad; often they serve our flourishing as personic animals. Of course, the person suffering doesn't like the suffering. But that's the point. It's the combination of feeling pain when burned and not liking the experience that makes it much easier to survive than would otherwise be the case; witness the precarious existence of those rare human beings who do not feel pain. The suffering serves our flourishing. It's for our good.

But now for the other face of suffering, the face that, for those who believe in God, proves deeply problematic. God intended that we, with the constitution God gave us, would flourish until full of years in the environment in which God placed us. Our constitution was designed with the environment in mind. And God blessed us—wished us well, wished each and every one of us well, not just wished us well as a species. But judged by reference to God's intent, things seem to have gone seriously awry. Sometimes a person's constitution is disordered in such a way that they suffer intractable pain and cannot flourish. More often, the fit between constitution and environment that was meant to serve our flourishing is ruptured. The food I need to sustain my animal existence is not available, so I die long before the fullness of years built into my design plan, suffering intensely from hunger. If you fall and only break an arm, that does not significantly inhibit your flourishing, and the suffering makes you more careful in the future. But if you die young from your injuries, I can expatiate as long as I have breath on the fact that this is a natural consequence of acting carelessly in the way you did, given the animal body that you have in this physical universe that is ours, that does not address the fact that your flourishing as a personic animal has been sliced off. Or, instead of finding sustenance and delight in the fellowship of your fellow human beings, you suffer neglect, indignity, abuse. Your human constitution, operating in our physical environment among personic animals of our kind, has not yielded your flourishing.

The divine experiment seems not to have worked out. I mean: the experiment of creating these strange boundary-crossing creatures, personic animals, endowed with freedom, placing them in this physical universe among fellow human beings, and doing so with the intent that such suffering as they endure would contribute to their flourishing until full of years, each and every one of them.

Back to our opening question. Is suffering good or is it bad? It all depends. Some of it serves our overall flourishing. Though suffering is intrinsically an existential No-saying to what causes the suffering, sometimes the fact that one's existence says "no" serves one's overall flourishing. But often that to which one's suffering says "no" is something that inhibits flourishing, one's own or that of someone else. Auschwitz, Cambodia, Somalia, Ukraine: mountains of suffering. The ambiguity pervasive in our existence includes suffering. Though suffering is not *per se* bad, though sometimes it conduces to our wellbeing, in suffering as a whole something has gone awry, horribly awry—in the causes of our suffering, in the extent of our suffering, in the depth of our suffering. What are we to make of this ambiguity?

There are theologians who would respond that I have gone much too fast, that I have made an unreflective lunge at the conclusion that suffering is ambiguous. I have not brought God into the picture. If I would expand my blinkered gaze and bring God into the picture, I would have to concede that there is no suffering about which one can correctly say, "It would have been better had this not happened." Suffering is not ambiguous. When God is brought into the picture, it becomes clear that all suffering is for our good.

This view comes in a number of different versions, the two most prominent being what is commonly called the *soul-making* theology of suffering, the other, what I will call the *aesthetic-totality* theology of suffering. My aim in this chapter is to present a theological account of the ambiguity of suffering. Before I do so, however, let us briefly consider these two alternative theologies of suffering. I will take John Calvin as representative of the soul-making theology and St. Augustine as representative of the aesthetic-totality theology.*

---

* A rather eccentric contemporary example of the soul-making theology of suffering is C. S. Lewis, *Problem of Pain*.

## The Soul-Making Theology of Suffering

Calvin writes:

> Whether poverty, or exile, or prison, or insult, or disease, or
> bereavement, or anything else like them torture us, we must
> think that none of these things happens except by the will and
> providence of God, that he does nothing except with a well-
> ordered justice. (*Institutes* III.viii.11)

What comes to expression in this passage is Calvin's incli-
nation toward so-called *occasionalism*—that is, the view that
God is the only true causal agent in reality. It's not the Covid
virus that caused my illness; God caused my illness on the occasion of my exposure to the virus. And as for the overall character of God's agency, God always acts for our good—with a
"well-ordered justice." Thus we get this passage:

> All the suffering to which human life is subject and liable are
> necessary exercises by which God partly invites us to repen-
> tance, partly instructs us to humility, and partly renders us
> more cautious and more attentive in guarding against the al-
> lurements of sin for the future. (*Commentary on Genesis* 3:19)

Our world is a vast reformatory, with God as superintendent.

In a passage quoted in the previous chapter, Calvin insisted
that we are not to follow those he called the "new Stoics" by

trying to alter our nature so that we no longer suffer. It is now clear what lay behind this comment. God's attempt to reform us by causing us to suffer presupposes the workings in us of a nature that yields suffering.

> If there were no harshness in poverty, no sting in disgrace, no dread in death—what fortitude or moderation would there be in bearing them with indifference? But since each of these, with an inborn bitterness, by its very nature bites the hearts of us all, the fortitude of the believing man is brought to light if—tried by the feeling of such bitterness—however grievously he is troubled with it, yet valiantly resisting, he surmounts it. (*Institutes* III.viii.8)

> Therefore in patiently suffering these tribulations, we do not yield to necessity but we consent for our own good. These thoughts, I say, bring it to pass that, however much in bearing the cross our minds are constrained by the natural feeling of bitterness, they are as much diffused with spiritual joy. (*Institutes* III.viii.11)

Suffering is God's gift to us. It is, indeed, a strange gift; we don't like the gift. But since it is for our good, we are to bear it with grateful patience. "If it is clear that our afflictions are for our benefit, why should we not undergo them with a quiet and thankful mind?" (III.viii.11). Regrettably, the gift does not always have its desired effect. Sometimes, instead of bringing about the moral and spiritual reform of the sufferer, it makes them bitter.

What caught Calvin's eye, in the picture he drew of God's stance toward suffering, is that God, out of love for God's creatures, causes us to suffer so that we may grow morally and spiritually. What catches my eye is that God employs my son's early death to bring about my moral and spiritual improvement. I find this grotesque.

Suppose that my suffering over Eric's death did indeed make me a better person. What about my son? What about the benediction God pronounced over him, that he would flourish until full of years? Should Calvin reply, "But he's better off now," I answer, "It was over *our earthly existence as animalic persons in this present world* that God pronounced a benediction." The shalom God desires for us is *embodied* shalom: flourishing here on earth until full of years.

## The Aesthetic-Totality Theology of Loss and Suffering

We can be assured, said Augustine, that God so governs what transpires in history as to bring it about that, when contemplating history in its totality, God delightedly recognizes it to be a glorious whole to which all that we do, and all that we undergo, make their contribution.

Mainly what motivated this view was, as we saw in the previous chapter, that Augustine, along with almost everyone else in antiquity, was persuaded that unremitting happiness, *eudaimonia*, constitutes the perfection of personal existence—and God's existence is, of course, perfect. But perhaps there were a couple of additional considerations working in Augustine's mind as well.

For one thing: Augustine, and the church fathers in general, were convinced that the longing of our hearts for *eudaimonia* will ultimately be satisfied by sharing in the life of God—a conviction that lies at the heart of the long-enduring tradition of contemplative Christianity. If the goal of our existence is happiness, and if our ultimate happiness consists in sharing in the life of God, then that life must itself be a life of peace and joy. If, upon entering into the divine life, we encounter vexation, disturbance, we would not have attained *eudaimonia*.

Second, Augustine, along with everyone in Christian antiquity who wrote on the matter, held that God is immutable, unchangeable. Given that conviction, it was impossible for Augustine to say that the divine joy, in the sharing of which lies our own *eudaimonia*, is a joy that God does not fully enjoy until the coming of God's perfected kingdom.

God's state is *apatheia*, apathy—a positive apathy, characterized by the steady unperturbed state of joy. God is aware of what transpires in the world, and God loves God's creatures. But nothing that happens in the world alters God's eternally blissful *apatheia*.

Augustine realized that Scripture speaks of the pity of God. But the pity of God, he says, must be understood as quite different from human pity. Human pity brings "misery of heart," whereas "who can sanely say that God is touched by any misery?" "With regard to pity, if you take away the compassion which involves a sharing of misery with whom you pity, so that there remains the peaceful goodness of helping and freeing from misery, some kind of knowledge of the divine pity is suggested."[*]

In another passage he writes:

God's repentance does not follow upon error, the anger of God carries with it no trace of a disturbed mind, nor his pity the wretched heart of a fellow-sufferer . . . , nor his jealousy any envy of mind. But by the repentance of God is meant the change of things which lie within His power, unexpected by man; the anger of God is His vengeance upon sin; the pity of God is the goodness of His help; the jealousy of God is that providence whereby He does not allow those whom He has in subjection to love with impunity what He forbids.[**]

So where is God in suffering? God brings it about that, whatever we do and undergo, when God contemplates the totality of what transpires in history, God is delighted. The source of my error, in concluding that suffering is ambiguous, was that I was abstracting episodes of suffering from their cosmic context, considering them in isolation, and then finding some

[*] Mozley, *Impassible God*, 105.
[**] Mozley, *Impassible* God, 106.

of them bad, evil. If one extracts a few measures from one of Bach's fugues and listens to those measures in isolation, one might well find them uncomfortably dissonant, ugly—depending on one's selection. That's because, when listening to them in isolation, one does not hear what precedes or what follows. Are we to conclude that, because these measures, when listened to in isolation, are distinctly unlovely, the composition as a whole would have been better had they not been included? Of course not. If, on the other hand, you had set yourself to listen to the whole fugue but some trickster, unbeknownst to you, had sliced out those bars that, in isolation, you found ugly, you would find the beauty of the whole painfully impaired. So too with the symphony of world history that God is conducting.

What caught Augustine's eye, in the picture he drew of God's stance toward suffering, was the joy and peace of God's eternal life as God contemplates the beautiful totality of things that God is bringing about, to which loss and suffering make their distinct contribution. What catches my eye is God remaining blissfully unperturbed while humanity drowns in misery. Is this what God had in mind when God blessed us, each and every one of us: that all our loss and suffering would find their place in the cosmic symphony that God is conducting? I find the idea grotesque.

## Suffering Gone Awry

Two traditional theological accounts of God in suffering: the soul-making account and the aesthetic-totality account. I find them both grotesque.

Who is the "I" that finds these two theologies of loss and suffering grotesque? A human "I," of course. But also a Christian "I." My self is not a self shaped by contemporary secular culture bumping up against the Christian gospel and finding it grotesque. My self is a self formed by Christian Scripture, finding these views intuitively repelling, and noticing that what motivated Calvin was not what leaps from the pages of Scripture but his commitment to radical occasionalism in his understanding of what happens in history, and noticing that what motivated Augustine was likewise not what leaps from the pages of Scripture but his commitment to a picture, pervasive in antiquity, of perfect personal existence.

So back to the ambiguity of suffering. Whereas Calvin was persuaded that the grief of a parent over the early death of a child is meant to enhance the moral and spiritual life of the parent and others, I am persuaded that, in the early death of one's child, suffering has gone awry. And whereas Augustine was persuaded that, if we could hear with God's ears what happened in Auschwitz, we would hear some measures in God's beautiful symphony of cosmic history, I am persuaded that what we hear in Auschwitz is suffering gone appallingly awry. Can these persuasions, these intuitions, be theologically articulated in fidelity to Christian Scripture? Where is God in suffering gone awry?

## Barth's Theology of Loss and Suffering

The theologian I have found most profound and helpful on this point is the German twentieth-century theologian Karl Barth. Barth's words are lyrically powerful; Barth was a poet among theologians. Accordingly, rather than offering my prosaic paraphrase of what he wrote, I will quote his own words. On first reading—and, for some passages, on additional readings as well—Barth's words are baffling; so rather than letting the reader struggle to grasp Barth's thought, I will offer my interpretation.

I propose first setting before us Barth's view as a whole in his own impassioned and astonishing words, and then offering my interpretation. The alternative, of quoting a bit of Barth, offering an interpretation of those words, quoting a bit more, offering additional interpretation, would result in a jarring alternation of colliding styles. Furthermore, to know what to make of any part of Barth's view, it's necessary that one have most of it before one; only then do things fall into place. The string of quotations will be long; given Barth's prolix style, there's no way around that. Even so, the passages quoted represent only a tiny fragment of Barth's full discussion of the topic.

The passages to be quoted come from a section of that

part of Barth's *Church Dogmatics* that deals with the doctrine of creation (III/3, 289-368). The heading of the section is translated into English as "God and Nothingness." The German term translated as "nothingness" is *das Nichtige*. "Nothingness" is as good a translation as English allows. But it's too smooth, too bland, too ordinary, too deficient in the connotations and evocative power of *das Nichtige*. So I will use the German. *Gott und das Nichtige* is the topic, God and *das Nichtige*.

There is opposition and resistance to God's world-dominion. . . . This opposition and resistance, this stubborn element and alien factor, may be provisionally defined as *das Nichtige*. . . . [T]hough unable to overwhelm and destroy the creature, it constantly threatens and disrupts it. . . . [I]t is not only inimical to the creature and its nature and existence, but above all to God Himself and His will and purpose. (289-90)

[B]etween the Creator and the creature . . . there is that at work which can be explained neither from the side of the Creator—nor from that of the creature, . . . and which yet cannot be overlooked or disowned but must be reckoned with in all its peculiarity. . . . We stray on the one side if we argue that this element of *das Nichtige* derives from the positive will and work of God as if it were a creature. . . . But we go astray on the other side if we maintain that it derives solely from the activity of the creature.

We must indicate and remove a serious confusion which has been of far reaching effect in the history of theology. . . . [T]here is a negative as well as a positive aspect of creation and creaturely occurrence. . . . Viewed from its negative aspect, creation is as it were on the frontier of *das Nichtige* and orientated towards it. . . . Yet this negative side is not to be identified with *das Nichtige*. . . . In creation there is not only a Yes but also a No; . . . not only clarity but also obscurity; not only progress and continuation but also impediment and limitation; not only growth but also decay; . . . not only beauty but also ashes; not only beginning but also end; not only value but also worthlessness. . . . [I]n creaturely existence . . . there are . . . success and failure, laughter and tears, youth and age, gain and loss, birth and sooner or later its inevitable corollary, death. . . . Yet it is irrefutable that creation and creature are good even in the fact that all that is exists in this contrast and antithesis. In all this, far from being null, it praises its Creator and Lord even on its shadowy side, even in the negative side in which it is so near to *das Nichtige*. (296–97)

What is *das Nichtige*, the real *das Nichtige* . . . ? In plain and precise terms, the answer is that *das Nichtige* is the . . . "reality" which opposes and resists God, which is itself subjected to and overcome by His opposition and resistance, and which in this twofold determination as the reality that negates and is negated by Him, is totally distinct from him. The true *das Nichtige* is that which brought Jesus to the cross, and that which He defeated there. (305)

Only God and His creature really and properly are. But *das Nichtige* is neither God nor His creature. Thus it can have nothing in common with God and His creatures. But it would be foolhardy to rush to the conclusion that it is therefore nothing, i.e., that it does not exist. God takes it into account. He strives against it, resists and overcomes it.... If we accept this, we cannot argue that because it has nothing in common with God and His creatures *das Nichtige* is nothing, i.e., it does not exist.... We must accept the fact that in a third way of its own *das Nichtige* "is." (349)

In the incarnation God exposed Himself to *das Nichtige* ... in order to repel and defeat it. He did so in order to destroy the destroyer. The Gospel records of the miracles and acts of Jesus are not just formal proofs of his Messiahship, of His divine mission, authority, and power, but as such, they are objective manifestations of His character as the Conqueror not only of sin but also of evil and death, as the Destroyer of the destroyer, as the Savior in the most inclusive sense.... It is a serious matter that all the Western as opposed to the Eastern Church has invariably succeeded in minimizing and devaluating, and still does so today, this New Testament emphasis. And Protestantism especially has always been far too moralistic and spiritualistic. (320–21)

What God does not will and therefore negates and rejects, what can thus be only the object of his *opus alienum*, of his jealousy, wrath and judgment, is a being that refuses and resists and therefore lacks His grace. This being which is alien and adverse to grace and therefore without it, is that of *das Nichtige.* . . . And this is evil in the Christian sense, namely, what is alien and averse to grace, and therefore without it. For it is God's honour and right to be gracious, and this is what *das Nichtige* contests. (353–54)

## Interpreting Barth

Thus far, Barth's words. What was he getting at? The clue, I suggest, is Barth's deep conviction that, judged by reference to God's intents and purposes, things have gone awry in God's creation. Barth rejects with passion the view that everything that happens has been brought about by God and that, accordingly, everything goes the way God omnipotently wants it to go. With equal passion he rejects the view that God brilliantly and effectively responds to everything we do and undergo so that, when the cosmic symphony God is improvising reaches its final cadence, everything that has happened will prove to belong just where and as it is.

There is, in creation, the disturbing phenomenon of *things going awry*. That, I suggest, is the meaning of the term *das Nichtige* as Barth uses it. The phenomenon Barth calls *das Nichtige* is the phenomenon of *things going awry.*

Things often go awry with respect to your and my intents

and purposes. That makes it clear that the full description of the phenomenon Barth calls *das Nichtige* is not just *things going awry* but *things going awry with respect to God's intents and purposes*. Thus it is that Barth says that *das Nichtige* exists only by reference to God's purposes, that it exists just by virtue of God saying "no" to it. Furthermore, it's not some neutral third factor. It's evil. By virtue of being what it is, namely, things going awry with respect to God's intents and purposes, *das Nichtige* is evil.

Given this interpretation of Barth's use of the term *das Nichtige*, everything Barth says falls into place and makes sense. Is there such a phenomenon? Does it exist? Yes, but not in the way that God and creatures exist; it has, as Barth says, a strange third mode of existence.

What, then, does Barth have in mind when he speaks not of *das Nichtige* but rather of "the negative aspect" of our creaturely life? I suggest that he has his eye on the negative yield of those two "systems" of which I wrote in the first chapter: the experiences that we find negatively charged and the events to which we respond negatively when we come to believe that they have occurred. Barth argues that there is nothing wrong with these two systems being components of our constitution and also nothing wrong, as such, with the negative yield of these two systems being part of our life on earth. Death when full of years is a negative aspect of God's good creation. Death when young is not; it is an assault of *das Nichtige*.

Thus Barth, in his own theological way, arrives at the same

conclusion I reached philosophically. Neither our constitution, nor the negatively charged experiences and beliefs that it yields, are, as such, to be identified with things going awry with respect to God's intents and purposes. To the contrary, as we saw earlier: it is, in general, good this way. What must be added, however, says Barth, is that these components of our constitution, and these episodes in our lives, constitute an openness to the assaults and ravages of *das Nichtige*.

God's stance toward things going awry with respect to God's intents and purposes is that—to use Barth's words—God "loathes" it, "abhors" it. Accordingly, God opposes it with—again to use Barth's words—"anger," "jealousy," "wrath." This opposition is God's "strange" work, God's *opus alienum*. God's "proper" work, God's *opus proprium*, is God's work of grace toward God's creatures. Toward *das Nichtige*, God shows no grace.

There is no necessity in God's having this side, no necessity in God's engaging in this strange work. Given God's pledge to act graciously toward God's creatures, and given the hostility to God and creature of *das Nichtige*, the *opus alienum dei* is indeed necessary. But God did not have to covenant Godself to God's creature; God's grace was free. It is out of freely pledged grace that God engages in this strange work of doing battle with *das Nichtige* for the sake of the creature.

Recall the Augustinian picture of God: in God there is nothing negative; God is uninterrupted blissful *apatheia*. By contrast, central in Barth's understanding of God is God's negative response to the ravages of *das Nichtige*; it is that which motivates God's strange work. God is "troubled," "disturbed," "angry." Listen to Barth's language, and as you listen, hear the contrast with Augustine:

> The incredible and real mystery of the free grace of God is that He makes His own the cause of the creature.... His grace as the basis of his relationship with His creature means that whatever concerns and affects the creature concerns and affects Himself, not indirectly but directly. ... Why is this? Because, having created the creature, He has pledged his faithfulness to it. ... He might have been a majestic, passive and beatific God on high. But He descends to the depths, and concerns Himself with *das Nichtige*. He would rather be unblest with His creature than be the blessed God of an unblest creature. ... He intervenes in the struggle between *das Nichtige* and the creature as if He were not God but Himself a weak and threatened creature. "As if"—but is that all? No, for in the decisive action in the history of His covenant with the creature, in Jesus Christ, He actually became a creature, and thus makes the cause of the creature His own in the most concrete reality and not just in appearance, really taking its place. (356–58)

So where is God in grief and suffering gone awry? God "would rather be unblest with his creature than be the blessed God of an unblest creature." God is there at our side, embracing our cause as God's own cause, angry because this assault on our shalom is an assault on God's embrace of our shalom, not willing to put up with the assault of *das Nichtige* but working to destroy this mysterious resistant factor in reality: the God of grace engaging in this "strange work."

## Going beyond Barth

But I wonder: is this all? Barth's language, when describing God's stance toward *das Nichtige*, is extraordinarily bellicose: wrath, anger, jealousy, loathing, abhorrence, opposition, battle. And surely that's right; God's response to Auschwitz is anger. But is that all that is to be said? Is there not something else in the picture Barth has drawn, of God and suffering gone awry, than God's bellicosity toward *das Nichtige*, something to which he has not drawn attention but that is implicitly there?

We understand large stretches of Barth's theology if we realize that he is firmly convinced that things have gone awry in God's creation with respect to God's intents and purposes. We understand even more of his theology if we realize that he was a relentlessly Chalcedonian theologian: at the center of his theology was the God-man Jesus Christ. Listen, once again, to a passage quoted above:

[God] intervenes in the struggle between *das Nichtige* and the creature as if He were not God but himself a weak and threatened and vulnerable creature. "As if"—but is that all? No, for in the decisive action in the history of His covenant with the creature, in Jesus Christ, He actually becomes a creature, and thus makes the cause of the creature his own in the most concrete reality and not just in appearance, really taking its place.

God became a creature, became Jesus Christ. And Jesus suffered, suffered like you and me. "He was acquainted with grief." In the suffering of Jesus, God suffered. Though Barth gives the point scant attention in the section of the *Church Dogmatics* that we are considering, this too is part of his picture of God in grief. It's implied by his Chalcedonian theology. When we look at Barth's picture of God in grief with this aspect of the picture at the center of our attention, something about God's relation to the creature comes into view other than God's bellicosity toward *das Nichtige*.

In our affliction, God is afflicted. Over our suffering, God suffers. Over our mourning, God mourns. Over our weeping, God weeps. What the believer sees when beholding the suffering of the God-man Jesus Christ—the thought makes one hesitate, I admit—is the suffering of God. What the believer sees when beholding the rabbi from Nazareth on the cross is not only human blood from sword and thorn and nail but the tears of God over the wounds of the world.

Suppose you have been tortured, physically tortured; and suppose you relate your experience to someone who has never been tortured nor experienced any other substantial grief or suffering. They have drifted happily through life—so far. Your description might well make them angry at the torturer; if so, then that person's anger at your torturer in response to your narration establishes between you and them a bond—a bond of the sort that would not exist between you and someone who blandly responded by remarking that torture too is part of the big picture, or between you and someone who responded by asking whether your suffering from the pain of the torture had deepened your spiritual life.

But now suppose that you relate your torture to someone who has also suffered deeply—perhaps has also been tortured. That person may also become angry at your torturer—once again, a bond. But something else happens as well. That person grasps what your experience of suffering was like in a way and to a degree that is unattainable by the first person, and who is accordingly able to share in it empathetically. Conversely, there is, in the inner experience of your listener, something that you are able to understand in a way and to a degree unattainable by someone who had not experienced deep suffering, and which you are enabled thereby to share in. There is between the two of you a bond of understood and shared suffering, going in both directions.

I am assuming that to understand to a significant degree what deep suffering is like you must yourself have experienced deep suffering. I can imagine someone replying that it's possible to understand deeply what deep suffering is like by imagining it, perhaps with the assistance of great literature. I don't believe it—though I have no argument other than my own experience. Before my own deep suffering over Eric's death I had grasped almost nothing of what it was like to experience such suffering. I had not imagined anything approaching what it was like. Not only did I not in fact come close to imagining what it was like; I don't believe I *could have* done so. Am I peculiar in this regard? I doubt it.

Though I think that, to one who has never experienced torture, a great deal of what the experience of torture is like is inaccessible, I do think that its dimension of suffering can be grasped to a considerable extent by someone who has undergone some other form of deep suffering. In general, the more similar another's suffering is to one's own, the more accessible it is to understanding what it is like, and thereby to share it empathetically.

Could God have understood what human suffering is like had God never experienced human suffering of any sort—had God only gotten angry over the assaults of *das Nichtige*? Could God have grasped what our suffering is like by imagining it?

Perhaps so. But in any case, these are idle speculations. For an implication of the Chalcedonian understanding of the identity of Jesus Christ is that God suffered our human suffering—that the person (*prosopon*) who was at once both divine and human experienced human suffering and grief. God understands what our suffering is like because God has experienced our suffering. But then the converse also holds: those human beings who have suffered deeply are thereby enabled to understand deeply a dimension of the life of God, and to share empathetically in that life. We are bonded in suffering.

I remarked that Barth was the poet among theologians. I find Calvin to have been the most suffering theologian among those I have read. I do not mean that historical research would show that he in fact suffered more intensively and extensively than any other theologian. I don't know about that. I mean that I hear more suffering expressed in his words, even when he is not expressly talking about suffering, than in the words of any other theologian I have read. A good deal of what he said about God and suffering I find grotesque and appalling; I have not concealed that. But listen to these words from the *Institutes*:

> While [the Son of God] dwelt on earth he was not only tried by a perpetual cross but his whole life was nothing but a sort of perpetual cross. . . . Hence also in harsh and difficult conditions, regarded as adverse and evil, a great comfort comes to us: we share Christ's sufferings. . . . How much can it do to soften the bitterness of [our] cross, that the more we are afflicted with adversities, the more surely our fellowship with Christ is confirmed. (III.viii.11)

We share empathetically in God's sufferings in Christ.

In the same passage, Calvin suggests, in characteristic fashion, that God causes us to suffer in order that we may share in Christ's sufferings and thereby be spiritually blessed. But may the converse be at least as close to the truth: that God suffered in Christ in order to share in our sufferings? Calvin says that as Christ passed "from a labyrinth of all evils into heavenly glory" (III.viii.11), so we may hope and expect our destinies to have the same shape, provided we share in Christ's sufferings. But Christ, in passing from suffering to glory, did not put his sufferings behind him; he did not disown them. He owned them, integrating them into the life of God. Perhaps when we, who have struggled to own our sufferings, are ushered into the life of God, we will find ourselves, for this reason, not alien but at home.

I conclude with a question whose answer I do not know. I can only live the question—painfully. I quote from my *Lament*:

> God is love. That is why [God] suffers. To love our suffering sinful world is to suffer. God so suffered for the world that [God] gave up [God's] only Son to suffering. The one who does not see God's suffering does not see [God's] love. God is suffering love.
>
> So suffering is down at the center of things, deep down where the meaning is. Suffering is the meaning of our world. For Love is the meaning. And Love suffers. The tears of God are the meaning of history.
>
> But mystery remains. Why isn't love without suffering the meaning of things? Why is suffering Love the meaning? Why does God endure [God's] suffering? Why does [God] not at once relieve [God's] agony by relieving ours? (90)

# POSTLUDE

In the course of my discussion of the penultimate draft of *Living with Grief* with about thirty men behind bars in the Richard A. Handlon Correctional Facility, students in the Calvin Prison Initiative, I put to them the question: "Is it possible to own one's grief redemptively in prison?" "Yes," they said, and they gave examples, many. The discussion was deeply insightful and emotionally intense. Five of the men subsequently wrote out their answer to my question. Following, with their permission, is what they wrote. My eyes have been opened to dimensions of grief, and to dimensions of owning grief redemptively, that I had never seen before.

For many, "grief" refers to the pain suffered as a result of loss: when we lose something we love, we experience the suffering of grief. I feel that this is an oversimplification. I believe that, beyond this traditional understanding, grief can also be experienced over loss that we are responsible for.

To clarify: many would agree with Wolterstorff's comment in our discussion, that the multifaceted grief of prisoners includes grief over the loss of the freedom they once enjoyed. But in my twenty-nine years of imprisonment, I have found that this sentiment is usually embraced only by those who refuse to take responsibility for their crimes. They claim victimhood and shut their eyes to the trauma they have inflicted upon others. I refuse!

Contrary to what "loss" implies, I did not wake up one morning to find that my freedom was suddenly missing. No one stole my freedom. I am not the victim of some elaborate plot to imprison me. No. The reality is that I *surrendered* my freedom when I exercised my own free will and agency and chose to take a life. I *relinquished* my freedom. My freedom was not snatched from me. When I committed my crime, I *owed* my freedom to society in exchange for the grief I created in others.

Have I experienced associated losses? Yes. For instance, over the course of my incarceration I have lost friendships, I cannot help care for my aging parents, and I no longer have the potential to be a father. These are losses that I grieve over in the traditional sense. But what I grieve differently—what I grieve most—is the pain and suffering that I am personally responsible for, the grief that I have introduced into the lives of others. My victim was not my only victim. She had a family, friends, peers, and an entire community that now grieve because of my actions. My own family, friends, peers, and community also grieve. They grieve for Debra, yes. But they also grieve for their loss of my former self. In one very permanent act of agency, I created a string of victims that now grieve in the traditional sense. In the light of this, my own traditional griefs do not even bear mentioning.

Here is where many mistake my grief as something else entirely. Many will say that I am writing about *regret*—not about grief. And yes, I do regret my crime. I regret many decisions I have made in life. But I do not simply regret the effect I have had on others. No. I *grieve* the effect I have had on others. To word it in the traditional sense: I grieve the loss of my own humanity—my tarnishing of the *imago dei*. I grieve the fact that I irreparably contributed to the brokenness of this world and affected others with such permanence that restoration is out of reach—only reconciliation is feasible.

So I will not join the ranks of those content to label their incarceration as a loss and ignore their responsibility for the communities we have maimed. Instead, I choose to honor each of my victims by living forward redemptively—my grief as a motivator and reconciliation as a hope. My hope for reconciliation is a silent, almost private, wish. It is not my main motivator. It is my grief and empathy for my victims that motivate me most. What is most important to me going forward is that I not perpetuate the harm and suffering that I am irrevocably responsible for.

Thus, "by re-ordering [my] love and commitments so that they more nearly reflect the true worth of things . . . [and] by deepening and expanding [my] understanding and empathy" (*Living with Grief*, 56), I will work toward mending the fabric of this world that I have rent. This I do in a variety of ways; for instance, I involve myself with numerous charitable activities that offer me an opportunity to crochet clothing for local shelters, grow vegetables for area food pantries, and build furniture and other goods to be auctioned off at various benefits. I have been a building trades tutor for nine years and a horticulture tutor for even longer. As a Calvin University graduate, I now serve as a teaching assistant to professors involved with the Calvin Prison Initiative and I mentor men with behavioral issues in the mental health unit here at Handlon.

These are just a few of my contributions in recent years—not in the interest of "works righteousness" but as a fulfillment of my responsibility to this world. That said, my primary mission today is to serve as an example to all those I encounter when engaging in the activities I mentioned. Prison, unfortunately, is an environment that discourages empathy. So whenever possible, I encourage it in others. I try to inspire my peers to examine the impact they have had on the world and help them understand the far-reaching effects of their actions.

Prompted by grief, I choose to live forward redemptively, making positive contributions to this world and encouraging others to do the same.

## Ahmad Nelson

I was recently moved from one housing unit to another because of the need for bed space. The unit I currently reside in is titled, by mental health, as Adaptive Skill Rehabilitation Program (ASRP). People in this unit are considered to have delayed cognitive development. After living in this unit for a couple of days I began to notice some of the mental abnormalities of those I came in contact with. After my interaction with them, I could not help but have mingled feelings of grief and compassion.

But it was not those observations that tilted the scale toward redemptive living in my case. It was when Larry X invited me to join a reading group of the men in the ASRP that my heart was expanded in the direction of service. The monotone of their voices, the slowness with which they moved from one paragraph to another, the constant assistance they needed to pronounce words—those radically fortified my empathy and increased my compassion and grief. But it's not enough to feel empathy and compassion, nor is it enough to grieve in situations of despair. The quintessential ingredients of these emotions are intended to turn them into actions, to change the situation. To live redemptively means to restore what was broken, to find what was lost. Simply put: to make things whole again.

To do that requires that one sacrifice time, effort, and personal pleasure for the benefit of others. That is what it means to live redemptively. It grieved God that the world was in the state it was in. So out of love and compassion for the world, God sent his only begotten son to lay down his life for the world. This is what Jesus did: he sacrificed his life.

Later that day I noticed how other Calvin Prison Initiative (CPI) graduates were engaging the ASRP population. I saw Potts resolving a conflict between two people; I saw Bryan expressing empathy to someone who looked depressed; I saw Rick helping someone with their GED; I saw Bobby showing people how to build a chess set out of cardboard. To me, this demonstrated the price of living redemptively: they were each selflessly sacrificing their personal wants and desires for the benefit of others. I saw living redemptively in practice, and I saw how grief can be turned into positive actions that effectuate change in a prison setting.

Last, I have witnessed the love my peers are showing to the people in this housing unit, and its positive impact. I have seen how their love reaches the pinnacle of what God wants for all human beings. In the prison environment, hostility runs high; at the heart of redemptive living in prison is a redemptive spirit of long-suffering and patience. This is what I have seen. I can testify to the effects of living redemptively in a prison setting. Not only is it possible to practice grief redemptively in an incarcerated setting; it is a model for how to live with grief redemptively on the outside.

## Brandon Strickland

The idea of practicing grief redemptively in an incarcerated setting is intriguing. The very idea that criminals could feel such a complex emotion as grief seems to me contrary to the commonly accepted wisdom of American society. It seems even more unlikely that our society would seriously consider the idea that prisoners would be committed to acting redemptively. Yet, it is this very idea, that those who are incarcerated not only feel a gamut of complex emotions but many of them also actively seek to live redemptively, that I want to propose.

When one considers what practicing grief redemptively would entail, it is necessary to consider the myriad of things over which those who are incarcerated grieve. Many of us grieve over the criminal acts we have committed and the harm we have caused to others. We deeply regret those acts, and would "take them back" if we could. Unfortunately, that is not how things work in this vale of tears. So many things, once done, can never be undone. One of the common cries of the repentant person is, "I wish I were not judged for the worst fifteen minutes of my life." Many of us who utter that cry try to live lives that repudiate those worst minutes of our lives with lives of redemptive service.

Our service cannot atone for our actions. We cannot serve our way out of our guilt and accountability. Most of the people who think they can somehow do enough stuff to make it all better are generally not very good people. They usually aim to get something for themselves out of their service. It is rarely for the good of those they have harmed, or for the good of the world. For this type of person, grief, if it is felt at all, is not lived redemptively. I have noticed that many people of this type seem to think that they are the only ones whose grief and suffering matter. They go through life seemingly oblivious to the effect they have on the world.

We create holes in the world every time we commit an offense against our fellow man. When we harm others in thought, word, or action, we create holes in creation. My friend and mentor, Professor Dale Cooper, claims that when we speak unkind words to others, we commit murder. We murder our brother or sister with our words. At first, this seemed to me an exaggeration; after all, the harm caused by words is not the same as physical harm, right? But then I began to think that maybe, in some ways, it is worse. It is in those daily interactions with others that we form our relationships, and those can be either life-affirming or life-destroying. I began to wonder how often I have murdered a part of someone with an unthinking cruel word.

I came to realize that by our unthinking words and actions, we create holes in people's lives. Sometimes, if this offense is small—a careless thought or word—we can try to make amends and fill the hole; however, we can never make it happen that things are as if that hole had never been created. Even if we obtain forgiveness, the memory of the small thing—the careless thought or word—remains. When the offense is large, such as a crime against another, it is unlikely that any action on our part will fill the hole we have created. In the most egregious cases, those holes will go on to create other holes, as those against whom we have offended struggle to live in strange new worlds that make little sense.

Contrary to popular belief, many of us who are incarcerated grieve over the holes we have created in the world. We grieve for our victims and for their families and communities. We grieve for our own families and all we have taken from them. We grieve for the lives that could have been, had we been more caring, more patient, more loving. It is out of that grief that we try to build lives of service. Some of us have been blessed to be part of the Calvin Prison Initiative, which has opened possibilities for redemptive living that many do not have.

However, do not think that those not in the Calvin Prison Initiative lie around wallowing in grief without acting. Prisoners who are trying to live redemptively find ways of living out their grief. Many take an active role in the prison church and spend themselves making certain that the services run smoothly; some spend themselves helping others learn to read or do basic mathematics; still others seek out the lonely and marginalized and help them negotiate the hostile world of the correctional institution. Every redemptive action, most of them unseen and unacknowledged, is a step toward filling a hole in another person's life.

The punch line is this: we cannot fill the holes we have created, but we can fill the holes others have created. We can be the person who helps another heal; that comes in very handy in prison, since so many of the people here are deeply wounded in body and spirit. It is not possible to overstate how important it is to have people working to make the prison a better place through practicing their grief redemptively. They are using their grief to heal others; and that alone changes the world. Not in large ways, not in showy ways that get a spot on the nightly news, but in ways that affirm the worth of those around them. It is the feeling of worth that is all too often missing in the lives of those around us. Not only in prison, but in society at large as well. Many of the men in prison who are practicing their grief redemptively recognize the ways in which they have contributed to feelings of unworthiness.

There is something incredibly human in our ability to empathize with others and to seek their good, not just our own. What matters is the willingness to practice grief redemptively regardless of the apparent success or failure of one's efforts. We may not see someone benefit from our actions; nonetheless, we may fill a hole left open and bleeding in someone's life. And we can do that anywhere, even in an incarcerated setting.

*Rick Reamsma*

*Question: Can you live your grief redemptively in prison?*

Looking around this prison, I see many folks living their grief redemptively. There are several areas where redemptive grief-living takes place. A short list would include earning a bachelor's degree from Calvin University, learning a vocational trade, training dogs for service, gardening for donations to the battered women shelters, mentoring the cognitively underdeveloped among us, assisting various recovery programs, and being active pastors, elders, deacons, and members of the various prison church services. These are just some of the visible areas where prisoners work to reconcile the relationship between themselves and the community. There are many other areas that are invisible. All these areas help us here in prison perform the painful work of doing surgery on our souls. The end result, hopefully, is that not only do we recover from the soul-surgery as strengthened and redeemed persons, but that society recognizes the transformation and accepts the healed soul back into its fold.

We can never go back to the moment of the grief we caused and refrain from doing what we did. We can, however, allow that grief to become the catalyst of recovery, redemption, and, ultimately, reconciliation. Navigating the path from espoused theology (thinking deeply) and embodied theology (acting justly) to lived theology (living wholeheartedly) is not an easy endeavor, at least not at first. Nonetheless, to the agents who redeem their grief and who experience reconciliation, renewal and flourishing abound. I am convinced that if we can reach the lived theology of soul surgery, the world will notice and give glory to God our father (Matthew 5:16).

*Question: Can you, a prisoner, identify, own, and redeem your grief redemptively as an individual, or does it require a community?*

I contend that the identifying and owning of grief by the prisoner has to take place individually. The prisoner has to put in the hard work of identifying the grief they have within themselves and the grief they have caused others—for example, the victim, the victim's family, the victim's friends and immediate neighbors, the victim's neighbors in the broader community, plus the prisoner's family, friends, and neighbors. Furthermore, the prisoner has to excise the minimizings and justifications they have created in their thinking, and take full responsibility for the grief they have caused, both in themselves and others. In short: they must fully own their role in the grief they have caused.

Only after the prisoner has identified and owned the many forms of grief they have caused can there be any true reconciliation. Only by doing this can the prisoner make room for communities to come in to support, encourage, and embrace the soul surgery that has taken place. For the repair of soul surgery to take place, one's humanity needs a support system geared toward rehabilitation and, ultimately, forgiveness. No matter how much has been repaired, the surgery does little good (and may make the prisoner bitter), if no one embraces the repair and recovery of the grieving individual, who is looking to pay penance to those they have grieved.

## Emil Sporcic

*Question: How do you as a prisoner own your grief?*

Having lost my mother just four days before writing these words, my grief is fresh and raw. My grief expresses itself in many ways, mostly as crying, laughing, and sleeping. One way I own my grief is by crying. Crying is typically taken as a sign of weakness in prison. I do not feel weak when my tears flow; I pay my mother honor when I shed tears for her death.

An important aspect of grief in prison is isolation. Prison is designed to isolate. I am locked away from my family. I cannot share with them my grief, my memories of our mother, the daunting task of making arrangements for the funeral. However, I am consoled by the fact that I am supported by other inmates, some of whom have earlier experienced grief like mine over the loss of a loved one, compounded by the walls of a prison. My grief is mine to feel in all its searing intensity. But as I deal with it, I rely on those others who understand the painful nuances of losing a loved one while incarcerated. I am not sure that I could carry this pain without their support.

*Question: Can you live your grief redemptively in prison?*

In my experience, prisons are not designed to rehabilitate. Prisons are society's toxic waste dumps for human beings. The purpose of the waste dump is to protect society from harm. No one cares about detoxifying the toxic waste. It is waste, after all.

Nonetheless, yes, I believe it is possible to live grief redemptively in prison. It is up to us, on our own, to live redemptively. In my case, I took something from my victims that I can never give back. Since I cannot repair the damage I have caused, I strive to "do good" in other ways. Previously, I put *my* wants before the needs of others. Now, I put others first. Previously, I lived a life of excess—far beyond my means. Now, I try to do everything in moderation. Previously, I did not care about the feelings of others. Now, I try not to be abrasive and hurtful to the people I encounter, and to lift up the spirit of my fellow inmates.

*Question: What are the conditions required to live redemptively?*

Jesus!

I was saved on October 14, 2014, at 7:30 pm in the Saginaw County Jail. Prior to that, I was feeling an immense amount of self-pity. After my electrifying encounter with the Holy Spirit, I came to realize that I was the villain in the story Jesus tells in Matthew 22:37–39 about how to live redemptively. "*You shall love the Lord your God with all your heart and with all your soul and with all your mind. This is the first and great commandment. And a second is like it: You shall love your neighbor as yourself.*"

Since Jesus has already provided the tools, it doesn't matter what tools the prison (or society) provides or does not provide. We are already equipped for the task at hand, and the Lord expects us to do it with love.

# BIBLIOGRAPHY

Augustine. *The Confessions.* Translated by R. S. Pine-Coffin. Harmondsworth, Middlesex: Penguin, 1961.

———. *On Christian Doctrine.* Vol. II, *The Nicene and Post-Nicene Fathers.* Translated by Philip Schaff. Grand Rapids: Eerdmans, 1976.

Barth, Karl. *Church Dogmatics.* III/3, *The Doctrine of Creation.* Translated by G. W. Bromiley and R. J. Ehrlich. Edinburgh: T&T Clark, 1961.

Calvin, John. *Commentary on the First Book of Moses, Called Genesis.* Translated by J. King. Reprint. Grand Rapids: Eerdmans, 1948.

———. *Institutes of the Christian Religion.* Translated by Ford Lewis Battles. Philadelphia: Westminster, 1960.

Lewis, C. S. *The Problem of Pain.* Sixth impression. London: Fontana, 1965.

Mozley, J. K. *The Impassible God*. Cambridge: Cambridge University Press, 1926.

Swinburne, Richard. *The Existence of God*. Oxford: Oxford University Press, 1979.

Wolterstorff, Nicholas. *Justice: Rights and Wrongs*. Princeton: Princeton University Press, 2008.

———. *Lament for a Son*. Grand Rapids: Eerdmans, 1987.

www.ingramcontent.com/pod-product-compliance
Lightning Source LLC
Chambersburg PA
CBHW030919150426
42812CB00046B/372